"This is the book anxious moth[ers need]. [With] refreshing honesty, Lara welco[mes us to trust the] sovereign hand of God, cling to [Christ's promises]. Equal parts convicting and compassionate, A Mother Held will be a balm to any mother's anxious heart."

—**Ashlee Gadd**, Founder of Coffee + Crumbs, author of *Create Anyway: the Joy of Pursuing Creativity in the Margins of Motherhood*

"As a mom of small children who struggles with anxiety, I found Lara's book to be validating as well as encouraging. The way she weaves truth with personal narrative drew me in from the moment I picked up the book. It's perfect for the mom who is weary and in need of the reminder that Jesus is holding onto her as she holds her children."

—**Brittany Allen**, debut author with Lexham Press

"In *A Mother Held*, Lara d'Entremont sketches an intimate portrait of a mom who is—like us all—deeply affected by life lived in a broken and fallen world, but who is also beloved and held strong by her merciful Savior. A Mother Held encourages all moms with the truth of God's goodness and faithfulness in the midst of the anxieties and fears of motherhood—something every mother can relate to."

—**Christina Fox**, author of *Idols of A Mother's Heart*, *Sufficient Hope: Gospel Meditations and Prayers for Moms*

"*A Mother Held* is a raw retelling of the hardest moments Lara has faced on her journey in motherhood. As I read Lara's honest stories of her struggle with anxiety, my own heart was comforted and reminded that God's steadfast love carries us when anxiety overwhelms us. You will leave this book knowing you are not alone in the battles you face, and you are never without hope—you are held by Christ."

—**Gretchen Saffles**, Founder of Well-Watered Women, author of *The Well-Watered Woman*

"Lara has woven together a lovely memorial of God's faithfulness, prompting me to consider his goodness within my own story. When fear and anxiety are great burdens, Christ is greater still. He is in every detail, and he cares for you, Mom. Be comforted by Lara's beautiful essays and reminded that you are a mother held by the Everlasting Arms."

—**Kristen Wetherell**, mother of three; author of *Humble Moms* and *Help for the Hungry Soul*

"Reading each of Lara's essays in this collection, the word that kept coming to mind was "tenderness". As a reader, it's a gift to be met with the tenderness of an author willing to share their struggles, and as an author, this is only accomplished when one takes care when telling her stories. Lara understands this, and the care with which she shares her stories, the tenderness with which she extends her hand to the reader, reads like mercy. This collection of essays is a treasure. "

>   —**Kris Camealy**, author of *Everything Is Yours: How Giving God Your Whole Heart Changes Your Whole Life*

"Lara writes with compassion toward herself, which extends to the reader who is struggling with all the woes and worries and ways of new motherhood. By revealing her own struggles with anxiety and depression, she removes their strength and is a welcome friend to other moms who may feel alone in those struggles. Lara's journey highlights the necessity for community and professional help, good books, nature, and most importantly, the abounding grace of Jesus."

>   —**Tresta Payne,** writer behind More Beautiful Than Necessary with Tresta Payne

"Lara d' Entremont offers readers a brave, raw, beautiful, and hope-laced telling of the hard journey that mothering can sometimes be. Her honesty is needed, not just by mothers of high need children, but all mothers who face the longed for but often wearying path of raising new human beings to grown ones. Lara's very telling of this story allows us each to find a framework for our own parenting experience and our deep need for an enveloping grace to hold us and give us hope."

>   —**Lancia E. Smith,** Publisher and Executive Director of Cultivating Oaks Press, LLC

A MOTHER held

LARA D'ENTREMONT

Lara d'Entremont

A Mother Held: Essays on Anxiety and Motherhood

Copyright @ 2023 by Lara d'Entremont

Published by Calla Press Publishing
    Texas Countryside
    United States 76401

All rights reserved. No part of this publication may be reproduced, stored in a retrieval system or transmitted in any form by any means electronic, mechanical, photocopy, recording, or otherwise without the prior permission of the publisher, except as provided by USA copyright law.

Cover Design: Publisher of Calla Press Publishing
First Printing, 2023
Printed in China

Unless otherwise indicated, Scripture quotations are from the ESV Bible (The Holy Bible, English Standard Version), copyright © 2001 by Crossway, a publishing ministry of Good News Publishers.
All emphases in Scripture quotations have been added by the author.

Trade paperback ISBN: 979-8-9888702-6-5

A Mother Held

To my husband, Daniel

Not only did you do everything possible to support this dream of mine from the very beginning, but you stood by me through every panic attack, every anxiety-filled night, and every valley of darkness. You promised to always stay, and you kept that promise. I love you.

Lara d'Entremont

Table of Contents

Foreword	8
Prologue	10
1. He Holds the Unborn	14
2. Not Just Morning Sickness	22
3. Breastfeeding and Thorns	29
4. An Identity Smothered in Diapers	35
5. Memorial Pieces of My Home	41
6. Grief and Joy In Tandem	49
7. Longing for Home	53
8. The Extra Hands and Feet I Need	58
9. When My Body Failed	62
10. Watching Deer	69
11. What If It's Me?	74
12. The Purpose of My Home	82
13. Learning Courage	90
14. No Gold Stars for Burnout	98
15. He Will Hold Me Fast	109
16. Overlooking the Valley	114
17. A Story Led Me Home Again	120
18. Eyes on Today	126
19. Given to Us and For Us	132
20. A Life Lived Out of Doors— Despite the Dangers	141
21. On Growing Old, Being Loved, and Becoming Real	147
Epilogue: I Look Toward	154
Acknowledgements	161
About the Author	165

Lara d'Entremont

Foreword

We all have dreams of what it will look like to carry and raise a child, shaped in part by our own experiences, and influenced in no small measure by the highlight reels of others' lives we are constantly scrolling. None of us are immune: every single woman begins her motherhood journey with expectations and aspirations—both for our children, and certainly for ourselves.

And then those precious miracles are placed in our arms, and reality jolts us into humility. Because who among us can say that motherhood is everything we imagined it would be; or that we are everything we thought we would be as a mom?

In *A Mother Held*, Lara gently and vulnerably walks us through her own stories of learning to be a mother, stories that any mom will resonate with in her own way. She writes about the crippling fear and worry that begins even before we know who our children are, and the difficulty of releasing the false sense of control we all cling to. She shares with openness about her weakness and God's strength, and how life continues to show her it takes the former for the latter to be made real.

Lara is a woman who writes with eternity on her mind, and that is what shines through in each of her thoughtfully crafted essays.

Lara d'Entremont

Lara does not shy away from the hard, but she has a beautiful and poetic way of reminding us all of the good. From anxiety to miscarriage, unexpected diagnoses and developmental challenges, and the sweetest moments of savoring the gift of a child's laughter, one cannot put down a story from Lara without seeing what she sees: a Sovereign and good God behind it all. Read these stories and be reminded that you are held—not by luck, merit, or any mustering of your own strength—but by the God who gives life, and plans to use yours, with all of its ups and downs and inside-outs, for His glory to a watching world.

– Katie Blackburn

Prologue

*You must depend upon
affection, reading, knowledge,
skill—more of each
than you have*

. . . . .

*Communicate slowly. Live
a three-dimensioned life;
stay away from screens.*

— Wendell Berry, How to be a Poet[1]

"I have so many fears," she said. "I fear miscarriage, so much so that I actually *want* the morning sickness to come—as crazy as that sounds," she continued, her eyes not meeting mine. "I just want to be excited about hearing the baby's heartbeat in a week, but instead I'm afraid of not hearing it at all."

That woman could have been a younger version of me.

The young woman and I sat on the couch in my living room, the late-setting, summer sun beginning to draw shadows across the floor. I kept my eyes on her, not wanting to look away or give any sign of distraction. I intimately understood the words this new bride uttered, and I knew she needed someone to hear her words and not just speak peace over her but tell her she was not alone.

As I listened to her fears and anxieties, I wanted to collect

---

[1] Wendell Berry, "How to Be a Poet," Poetry Foundation, July 31, 2018, https://www.poetryfoundation.org/poetrymagazine/poems/41087/how-to-be-a-poet.

every story from motherhood when my anxiety retold the same narrative to me. Not because those stories are all ones of victory and happy endings and would thus reassure her that all would be well for her too. But because I know the power of stories—both fictional and real—to not only tell a person they are not alone but to give them an image of hope to grasp onto and a light to lead them out from the caves of despair.

I didn't want to gather these stories to give her a step-by-step plan for conquering the obsessive worries and fears that pervade motherhood—I still wrestle with these each day. I'm far from equipped to counsel others on how to run with abandon from this unique kind of suffering.

That's why this is not a book on how to not be an anxious mother. It's not about believing and declaring the future you want and listening for promises from God. This collection is for the mom who wonders where God could be as her pulse pounds like a woodpecker's beak, and questions how she'll ever be able to trust in God again.

I didn't write all these stories to be affirmed or to show how hard my walk in motherhood for these short five years has been. Instead, I tell these stories to witness to you God's sovereign, redemptive hand through every terror, toil, and celebration. I want to show you that the same God who holds the power that wrought the world into being and flung the stars across the inky blackness of the sky likewise holds you in his palm and cares for you as his child. The One who predestines an asteroid's drift through space likewise engraved you on his palm and wrote your particular story for his glory and your good.

A Mother Held

In Wendell Berry's poem *How to be a Poet*, he says that a poet (and I'd argue writers in general) must read well and live a three-dimensional life. I placed a piece of this poem at the head of the chapter because I strive to live by those words whenever I write, and I believe this book is the fruit of that.

Since I became pregnant with my first son, a version of this book has lived on my laptop. As I sat a belly's distance from my desk, I wrote a proposal about a life with anxiety and how God's attributes comforted me. Back then, only a tiny portion of motherhood took up that story. I remember listening to podcasts, taking courses, and chatting with experts. I outlined chapters while the toddler I babysat slept upstairs.

Despite how much time, hand cramps, and headaches I suffered, that book proposal received rejection after rejection after rejection. I sulked a lot, and I wondered at all the time I had wasted. Yet a writer friend spoke seemingly prophetic words that comforted me: "This is not wasted, Lara," she said. "You've learned so much through this. And perhaps one day you'll get to write this book a few more years down the line when you'll have more experience and goodness to offer your reader through the challenges of motherhood."

I smiled a little and tried to find courage in her words. Little did I know how true her words would become.

Over the past six years, God led our family through both fields of flowers and gentle waters along with dark valleys that seemed to have no end in sight, all within the framework of motherhood. My lifetime of anxiety climbed around me like the briars of a rosebush, and I at times struggled to see my Shepherd at all—sometimes I had my eyes closed and other times the darkness had grown too inky black to see anything at all.

Yet this isn't the only three-dimensional life I believe Berry referred to. In the midst of that, I've walked alongside other women in the darkness of their anxiety amidst their motherhood journey. I typically didn't have advice for them but I had stories, and I offered up as many as I could tell to assure them they had not lost their minds and that God would indeed carry them through too—not because of their courage (because I knew I had so little), but because of his love and grace.

Berry also mentions "affection, reading, knowledge, and skill." You'll notice throughout this book that I make literary references and most chapters begin with a poem. There is nothing new under the sun, as the preacher of Ecclesiastes declared, and so I look to the literature created by both new and old writers to guide us. Along with my own story, I've woven the stories of fictional characters and the wise thoughts of others of the faith because I must depend on more wisdom than I have within myself.

This is what I hope for you to hear in every single essay: Your Savior remains faithful when the stomach-churning fears come. He's trustworthy and beautiful, even when your most catastrophic fears and thoughts come true before your eyes. He remains just as close and near when you celebrate and when you grieve. He does not abandon his children but watches them as he does every sparrow in the sky.

These stories are not about me and my family; they are about the God who carried us through—and I want to train your eyes to see him in your story too. At times these stories might read a little bit like the book of Esther—God's name may only be mentioned once, but that doesn't mean he's not there turning the hearts of kings and peoples and guarding his beloved. As I have found eyes to see my Father at work in my story with a backward glance, my prayer is that you'd learn how to see God right now, not just in hindsight. May you know with every essay in this collection that you are one of many mothers held by God.

1
He Holds the Unborn

> *Whatever our particular calamity or adversity may be, we may be sure that our Father has a loving purpose in it. As King Hezekiah said, "Surely it was for my benefit that I suffered such anguish" (Isaiah 38:17). God does not exercise His sovereignty capriciously but only in such a way as His infinite love deems best for us.*
>
> — Jerry Bridges, Trusting God: Even When Life Hurts[2]

I stared in disbelief at the no-longer-blinking pregnancy test. "What does that say?"

My husband jumped up from the bathroom floor and opened his arms to embrace me. "You're pregnant, Lara! We're going to have a baby!"

He wrapped me in his arms with a smile on his face that reminded me of the one I saw when he first laid eyes on me walking down the wedding aisle. I smiled too but hid the tension of it against his neck. My heart and mind raced. *How can it be? How did it happen so easily? How am I pregnant so quickly?* And then, the inevitable thought, *What if I miscarry?*

---

[2] Jerry Bridges, *Trusting God: Even When Life Hurts*, 2nd ed. (Colorado Springs, CO: NavPress, 2008), 8.

This irrational, stomach-churning, obsessive, heart-pounding anxiety was nothing new to me; my anxiety has manifested in various ways. As a young girl, I spent many hours crying in the bathroom terrified to vomit, shrieking in fright whenever the sensation of bile rose in my throat.

I thought maybe age would take this beast from my life. It didn't. Perhaps a healthy lifestyle of clean eating and exercise would kill my anxiety. It still thrived.

Maybe when I finally became a truly born-again believer my anxiety would be done away with. It wasn't.

I believed that when my husband slipped that glittering, rose-shaped diamond ring on my finger at the altar, my anxiety would vanish with my singleness in a moment. It simply grew with new angles to prod me.

At twenty-one years old and pregnant with my first, I expected this beast to be nothing but a slain carcass. Yet, I was still like that small, young girl in the bathroom.

Shortly following the positive test, nightmares followed. At least once a week, I awoke in bed with tears trickling down my cheeks and my body covered in sweat. Images of miscarriages and stillbirths haunted me, seeming real even after I opened my eyes.

One of those nights, Daniel sat up next to me and wrapped his arms around me. "It's okay, honey, it's okay. It was just a dream."

I touched my hands to my stomach. "Is my baby okay?"

Rubbing my back, he nodded. "Yes, the baby is safe in your belly."

The nightmares filled the first few weeks of pregnancy, leaving me more exhausted than all the changes morphing my body into a mother. They gave the "what ifs" a poignant edge of realness and likelihood. *What if it comes true... How will I cope? What will I do?* Anxiety swallowed the expectant wonder that motherhood should have wrapped me in, like a vicious beast.

Because of this, I clung to the hope of reaching my second trimester. Whenever my fears of miscarriage overwhelmed me, I reminded myself, *Once you reach the second trimester, you can rest knowing your chances of miscarrying are lowered significantly.*

But that first trimester passed, and my fears refused to fade.

Although my chances of miscarriage lowered, the possibility still existed. Such is the morbid and hopeless thought-life of the anxious: If there's a possibility for tragedy, despite how low the likelihood, the fears still assail to the most catastrophic degree.

My new motto became, *Once the baby is born and out of my fragile womb, I'll be able to protect him or her.* Though still a long six months away, it was the only hope I thought I had left. Once the baby was out, he or she was then in my control, and I could monitor and care for him or her.

This thought comforted me for a while, but it wasn't long before that reassurance was ripped from my grip as well. I soon worried about the many situations where my child's safety would be threatened outside my womb. My arms can't shield my child from disease. My weak body will need sleep, meaning I must leave my child alone in their crib, unguarded. Someday, my child will grow up and leave the house, where my eyes can no longer oversee their every movement and complexion change or hear their breath come in and out.

My eyes burned from tiredness one evening as I stood next to my husband at the sink drying the dishes he set in front of me without looking at them. The sun slanted over my face from the window as I stared at the grass reflecting a golden hue from the evening light. At first, images of our child running laps barefoot in the yard came to mind, causing me to touch my stomach with a sense of awe. Then, as a car rattled down the road, my hand clenched at the image of that same child lying crumpled in the road.

"I am never going to be able to keep our baby fully safe, fully protected, ever," I whispered.

Daniel turned to me, a soft smile on his face. Knowing my nightmares and fears, he replied, "No, you can't. But God can. God will do what he sees best for our baby. God is sovereign and good."

I wanted that truth to be in my heart. I knew it so well in my mind—I could show you the Bible verses and expound on the character of God, but my heart still fought to cling to those truths.

Each day after that conversation, I held onto those words like a life-saving rope. *God is sovereign and good.* Each time a fear popped into my head, each time a nightmare awoke me from sleep, I told myself, *God is sovereign and good.* Some days I whispered it through tears and prayed, *God, help me to believe you are sovereign and good. Help my unbelief.*

Exhaustion wearied my mind and body—both from pregnancy and wrestling with anxious thoughts. When will it be done? Will it *ever* be done?

Weeks following that positive test, I dragged my feet up the stairs to the bathroom to get ready for the day, grogginess still settled over me. As I got undressed, I saw red in my underwear.

"Daniel, there's blood!"

Daniel ran partially dressed from our bedroom. He stumbled to a stop in the doorway. "What?"

"There's blood, Daniel! What should I do?"

He handed me my phone from the vanity.

"Call Melody."

I nodded and clicked her name in my contacts. She was my neighbor down the road, the wife of my pastor, and my dearest friend. The phone rang. The voice of her husband greeted me. I swallowed hard against the lump in my throat, and my voice cracked and shook every word. "Can I talk to Melody, please?"

A few minutes later Melody answered. "Hello?"

Sobs wrenched out of me. "Melody, I'm bleeding." I sucked in the air to finish my sentence.

"I don't know what to do."

"Okay, I'll find the prenatal clinic's number." She quickly found the number and relayed it off to me while Daniel typed it in his phone.

Before she hung up, she said, "We will be praying. Please call or text us at any time if you need anything."

I barely murmured a thank you before hanging up.

We called the clinic, which told us to make our way to the emergency room at the hospital. I gathered a phone and charger; we had an hour-long drive ahead of us.

I kept my hand securely on my husband's leg for the entire drive. The silence felt like a soaked towel over our heads. Then I broke down sobbing and whispered, "How much longer?"

Daniel, amid thick silence, said, "No matter what happens, God is good."

The hour-long drive and the ninety-minute wait at the hospital for blood work ticked by like a slow metronome. Part of me desperately wanted to know the results while another part of me wished I could sit in that waiting room forever in denial. I wanted to cling to the hope that this was normal and nothing to fear, but such hopeful thinking scared me. If I dared to hope, I knew the grief would cascade that much stronger. I longed to comfort my husband, but I didn't even know how to comfort myself.

Despite the anguish and turmoil that clattered in me, I forced myself to hold onto that one phrase Daniel said: No matter what happens, God is good.

Hours later, the door to our waiting room swung open. The nurse who had first heard my case called me. "This way, sweetheart."

Both terror and relief filled my heart as I walked through the doors and into the little examining room. Relief washed over me that my wait for answers must be drawing to a close, but fear seized me at the thought of what those answers could be.

The doctor came in and shut the door behind him. His easy posture and kind face helped ease my panic a bit.

He brought a stand carrying a computer and a few tools.

"Have you had an ultrasound already for this pregnancy?"

I nodded and told him it was a few weeks ago. "Okay, I'm going to go check those quickly and then I'll come back so we can do one here."

Maybe I would get to see my baby, but maybe I wouldn't see anything at all. Excitement and panic flooded me.

He came back and set everything up for the ultrasound. I pulled up my tank top and tucked a towel over my jeans. As he gelled my stomach and placed the ultrasound probe on me, I turned my head to stare at the cold yellow wall. I didn't want to see my fears become reality. I couldn't bear to see an empty screen.

I listened to the seconds tick by on the wall clock. The doctor broke the silence. "Oh, look at that, a sweet baby moving in there."

My heart pounded. I turned my head and whispered, "Really?"

"Yeah, take a look."

He turned the screen to face me and I watched as a tiny gray figure of a baby moved on the screen. My body trembled as tears ran down my face.

"My baby is okay?"

He smiled. "Yes, everything is fine. Your blood test came back with the proper numbers, your baby is the right size, and all looks well inside."

I wiped away tears and did my best to hold still despite my sobs as he finished the ultrasound, showing me the baby's head, spine, and sweet heartbeat. I watched the screen through glassy eyes and whispered a prayer of gratitude in my heart.

As we drove home, I believed this test of faith had sanctified me completely. Having gone through this and having fought to trust in God through it, my anxiety would finally be slain. Yet are any of our battles and struggles upon this earth ever finished like that?

A Mother Held

A few weeks later, I sat in the darkness of the car, only the street lamps and cars streaming in light for us as we drove. We were quiet, as we usually were when I voiced my latest anxiety. Outside, the deep purple clouds covered the sky like a window blind, only revealing a small portion of the sky at the horizon. The stars and moon stayed well hidden, so I kept my eyes fixed on that small portion of the exposed sky as I spoke.

"It's just hard, always being afraid," I whispered. "Last week, I loved feeling those gentle kicks in my belly. It always came as a pleasant surprise while I sat on the couch or lay in bed. Now, it's like I'm always watching and waiting with fear, wondering, 'Was that movement? Did the baby move? When was the last time I felt movement?' I'm just tired of constant fear."

I had longed for those sweet kicks and a rounded belly. Yet when I finally felt them, it wasn't at all what I had hoped for—instead of a joyfully fluttering heart waiting quietly and expectantly, I felt like a stalked animal constantly watching for those kicks to reassure me my child still lived. That visit to the hospital for harmless bleeding was not the last; my pregnancy seemed to be filled with hospital trips for unknown bleeding, random cramping like the pain of contractions, unbelievable backaches, odd heart palpitations, and all the worries that accompany those.

Like that day in the kitchen overlooking the front yard, I continued to be reminded that even when my little one finally arrived, my worries wouldn't dissipate. Even once he was finally freed from my fragile womb and I could hear his breathing stop, see his complexion change, feel his heart, check his temperature, I still couldn't grasp control in my fist for his little life.

My suspicions proved true. I birthed my little boy a day before his due date, and as I struggled to gently pull a shirt over his big, vein-covered head and dreamt of dropping him, I knew the worries were far from over. When he had his first cold, I gnawed my lip raw on the way to the doctor's office. When he had his first fever I cried from the guilt of not realizing something was wrong earlier (and fearing I had noticed too late). When he ate his first puréed meal, I suffered a headache the rest of the night contemplating what that butternut squash might do to his digestive system.

    I am in no less or more control now than I was before he was born. That baby's life is still in God's hands as much as it was then. Though I can cuddle him in my arms, place him on a doctor's table, and stick a thermometer in his armpit, they are only a mere perception of control. As my sweet baby grows, and eventually grows out of my arms, he will always fit in God's palm—and that is the safest place for him to be, I'm striving to believe.

2
Not Just Morning Sickness

Love took my hand, and smiling did reply,
Who made the eyes but I?
Truth Lord, but I have marred them; let my shame
Go where it doth deserve.
And know you not, says Love, who bore the
blame?
My dear, then I will serve.
You must sit down, says Love, and taste my meat:
So I did sit and eat.

— George Herbert, *Love*

"Lara, I think you've lost some weight."

My mother-in-law's words were a stake in my heart, though I knew they were never meant to be. I finished zipping my jacket over my tiny baby bump. "Really? Maybe it's just this jacket making it look that way," I lied.

She verbalized the fear I had pushed away all week: I'm not gaining the weight I'm supposed to.

Morning sickness made an appearance nine weeks into my first pregnancy. Though I had not thrown up yet (and hadn't vomited since childhood), each morning nausea greeted me and stayed all day. For most, this would be considered easy—*at least you aren't throwing up everything you try to eat*, they'd reply.

But for me, the mere thought of vomiting paralyzed me.

My phobia of throwing up is my earliest memory of anxiety. After my first experience with the flu as a young girl, the thought of vomiting gave me a visceral reaction.

I would collapse into panic attacks—crying, screaming, sweating, shaking—anytime my stomach began to gurgle. This fear became so strong that at times I refused to eat at all so I wouldn't have food in my stomach to vomit.

This fear controlled me. I refused to leave the house because I might be put in a situation where I would need to eat, or I might arrive at my destination, hours from the comfort of my home, and become sick. This fear kept me from eating and receiving the nutrients I needed. My phobia instilled anxiety in my mother as she watched me each meal time wondering if I would make it through. I hated this fear and what it did to me, but I was a powerless slave to its chains.

The car ride with my mother-in-law was quiet as I nibbled on a saltine. *This is not what I pictured pregnancy to be like.* Pregnancy was supposed to be exciting, full of wonder-filled surprises and sweet kicks in my belly. Instead, mine was filled with misery—reminders of the anxiety I had yet to conquer fifteen years later as a grown woman. I felt like a weak child again, helpless to a fear that still held me in its grips.

God, why can't I be free from this, even still? I prayed. I wondered and questioned with each silent plea: *If I can't conquer this anxiety, am I ready for motherhood? How will I raise a courageous child, who can trust God in the unknown, while I still fight against this anxiety? What kind of believer am I if I can't catch a grip on this single struggle?*

During my morning sickness, I spent many days curled up in a ball on the couch. Writing took too much energy for my tired brain and housework felt like a workout. I resorted to reading books, online articles, and listening to podcasts. As I did, I sought to dig up every bit of biblical information I could about anxiety and phobias.

A Mother Held

As I listened to and read Christians relate either the stories they'd witnessed or the ones they had lived, I heard over and over about people who defeated anxiety like a dragon with a single slash of their sword to the heart.

Maybe God's love for me had waned because I continued to give way to anxiety. Each day became a battle to believe the faithfulness of God I knew. I regularly lay on the couch with tears streaming down my face, feeling chained to cushions. *God, where are you? Are you still faithful, even still?*

We often long to hear these stories of conquering; they give us hope that we could one day do the same. Yet for me, a twenty-something-year-old young woman who had faced this same phobia and anxiety disorder her entire life, these stories evoked hot tears and frustration. Why would our good and just God give them freedom from their struggle while still allowing me to be crippled by fear?

Many of these stories contained prompts for the listeners to follow their lead and immerse themselves in Scripture about God's trustworthiness or do the homework given to them by counselors. Yet I *had* read every book I could find on anxiety, fear, and worry from a biblical worldview. I prayed and asked others to pray for me. I went to the doctor and had blood work done. I did the exercises, the workbooks, and memorized the Bible verses. Why did those in the stories I heard overcome while I remained stuck? This was the persistent question that kept me turning and doubting.

There had to be something wrong with me—God had abandoned me because of my spiritual immaturity—and no one could ever find out.

I kept this fear of mine a secret throughout the pregnancy. I wanted to stuff it under lock and key and bury it deep in the forest under moss and knotted tree roots. No one could know, let alone *see*, what a fool I became when nausea overtook me. If they knew, if they saw, what would they think of me? Horror would mark their faces. They'd be ashamed to know me—just like other people in my life had been when they found out. I couldn't hide the fear, so I hid myself. I didn't eat at other people's houses because meal times were the best candidate for my fear to rear its head. I stayed home from church potlucks. I never invited people to come visit me.

Part of me longed to share my fear with someone other than my husband, even to simply find someone else to share this burden with so he didn't have to carry as much. But I needed to know they would react well—they wouldn't laugh, ridicule, or slander me behind my back. They wouldn't declare I was "acting the fool" like my father would or tell me "to behave myself" as my first-grade teacher did.

Yet I couldn't rely on that. I couldn't rely on anyone. I learned that years ago.

In grade one, I was in the throes of an intense season of anxiety. My fear of vomiting led me to eat infant-sized portions, which in turn made my stomach more nauseated and created more anxiety. I feared leaving home for any length of time because I might feel sick, which made going to school a terrifying endeavor.

One morning I had a panic attack. Being quiet and shy, I hated to draw attention to myself, but I needed help. I felt as if I was going to throw up, I couldn't breathe, and my whole body shook. I crept over to my teacher who was bent over at another student's desk. As my jaw trembled, I opened my mouth to speak to her.

The words had barely left my mouth when she spun around. "Goodness, Lara!" she yelled. "You need to stop with this foolishness! There are people here with real problems! You need to grow up and go sit down!"

The whole classroom fell silent. I simply wanted to disappear.

I only nodded my head, wiped the tears from my face, and returned to my seat.

Over and over again, I found people who responded in the same way to my anxiety. "She needs to stop acting like a fool!" my father said. "My child just vomits and goes back to bed—none of this nonsense!" a family friend scoffed. "She's just looking for attention; she'll grow out of it eventually," my childhood doctor said with a shrug. "Don't you realize throwing up isn't that big of a deal?" a friend said with a laugh.

I learned how to suffer high levels of panic attacks within my mind so no one would see. Over the passage of time during my elementary and high school years, I came up with various ways of lying about panic attack symptoms. "This classroom is cold," I said as I shook with fear. "I had a big breakfast," I murmured as I tucked my uneaten lunch away. "I fell in the gravel," I replied when they asked about the wounds in my hands from clenching my fists too tightly. "It's just my period," I whispered as I hunched over from severe, anxiety-induced stomach cramps.

For years, I believed that nobody should be allowed to see my inner life because no one is safe—every person will use my weaknesses against me, so I must hide them.

As my young heart watched even believers treat me with such contempt and mockery, I knew God must see me this way as well—which was more crushing and terrifying, because nothing can be hidden from him.

Before my pregnancy, I started working for my pastor's wife who had a five-year-old, a two-year-old, and newborn twins. Despite my morning sickness, I forced myself to plow forward with this commitment—we needed the money, and I refused to show that this morning sickness had weakened me in any way. With my cold fingers stuffed in my pockets, I trekked up the long driveway past the church and into the parsonage. Each morning I let myself in, greeted them, and got my to-do list that lay on the kitchen counter, either in paper form or on the whiteboard.

As I walked into their house that day, my stomach still tumbled. My husband left late for work because I had curled up in the bathroom in terror that I would vomit. The nausea had since passed, but the weak feelings of anxiety still dwelled. A shock of fright electrified me as I met both my pastor and his wife at the door. They were lacing up sneakers and pulling hats on their heads. I had hoped to avoid them for at least the first thirty-five minutes.

I knew before he posed the question what he would ask. "Good morning! How are you today?"

I fidgeted with my phone in my pocket.

I could lie to my pastor's face and put on a sweet smile, or I could tell the truth as I am called to do—even when it hurts (don't think I'm super pious; he had recently preached a sermon on this very topic).

I let out a long huff of air. "Not that great today," I said through a strained smile and laugh. For some reason, I believed he might leave it there.

He furrowed his face. "Why's that?"

Heat rose to my cheeks. I swallowed against the gagging sensation. "Well, I thought I was going to throw up this morning, and that terrifies me, so I had a panic attack, and now I'm still not feeling the greatest," I blurted.

I wanted to swallow every word. My eyes tilted to the tile floor. *You're so, so stupid. You know what this means—it's the pastor and his wife. Can you imagine the judgment—*

His wife piped up. "That's not fun. I'm sorry to hear that. Do you think you're feeling up to the housework today?"

My head shot up. No judgment. No criticism. Just... *sympathy*.

"You know," my pastor continued, "if you ever just want to come over and lay down in the guest room, you're more than welcome to."

I blinked. My mouth opened and closed, trying to wrap itself around words. I imagined my gaping mouth resembling a fish gasping for air on land. "Th-thank you."

Isn't this what George Herbert showed through his poem about the love of Christ? We see the feast and shy away—how could we ever partake of such a meal with such a King? We're unworthy, we're too sinful, we're too filthy, we're too broken. Yet despite our repeated turning away in shame, he beckons us to return. "You must sit down, says Love, and taste my meat." How else can we respond to such a command of the King? "So I did sit and eat."

3
Breastfeeding and Thorns

We are like sheep gone astray, and know not which way to return, until we hear the Shepherd's voice. Can these dry bones live to God in holiness? O Lord, You know; and we cannot know it, except we learn it of You. We are like sheep gone astray, and know not which way to return, until we hear the Shepherd's voice. Can these dry bones live to God in holiness? O Lord, You know; and we cannot know it, except we learn it of You.

— Walter Marshall, *The Gospel Mystery of Sanctification*

"That's liquid gold right there," the nurse said, taking the few ounces of breastmilk I had pumped to store away in the fridge. To me, breastmilk felt more like fool's gold—it had all the shine of real gold but the speed in which it slipped away made me question all the labor it required, especially having already labored a child into the world.

During my first few weeks with my newborn baby, sleep was a faraway dream. I resembled a factory dairy cow, and everything smelled like breastmilk (both fresh and rotten). Life consisted of breastfeeding, sterilizing supplies, washing and folding burp cloths, and scrubbing spit up from every inch of my home (even on the baseboard and fridge). I felt claustrophobic, tied to a nursing pillow, and smothered under a nursing cover. My milk ducts frequently clogged and turned into mastitis—a painful infection that crippled me like the flu.

Everyone said breastfeeding came naturally. Yet bleeding nipples, nipple shields, and milk spraying on my shower wall felt unnatural. Hormones created turbulent emotions, adding to the difficulty of breastfeeding with snotty tears.

I knew the first sin, the fall in the Garden of Eden, seeped into every aspect of life, including motherhood (Gen. 3:16). This meant that what was supposed to come naturally—uniquely crafted, warm milk from a mother's chest—now came with its own thorns and thistles. Milk turns pink from blood. Infections, bacteria, and disease invade this bond between mother and child. What was created to be natural and simple now became barricaded by multiple possible obstacles.

Yet as I looked around, it seemed other mothers got to experience a glimpse of the Garden of Eden while they breastfed. A mom with twins nursed and read books to her homeschooled son. Another mom latched her infant in a matter of seconds. I both grieved and envied.

This rightly felt grief blocked out the gospel. Despite my struggles, I clung to breastfeeding because I saw my ability (or inability) to breastfeed as accruing points towards the "good mom" grade. *If I don't breastfeed, my baby won't be as successful as other children. If I don't breastfeed, I won't be able to hold my head high at the mom's group on Tuesdays. If I didn't breastfeed, I didn't try hard enough. If I don't breastfeed, I've failed as a mother.*

But nothing about breastfeeding came naturally. I took every bit of advice and technique the nurses gave me, yet it seemed neither I nor my son knew what we were doing; he latched better to a finger than to my breast, and I needed a nurse to latch him every single time—and each time he fell off. Our week-long stay in the hospital had nothing to do with complications from birth or my medical concerns with my son; rather, my ineptitude to latch him to my breast kept us there.

Finally, on the seventh day, I latched him and kept him on for an entire feeding.

An hour later, I walked into our dark living room for the first time since we left for the hospital. A sliver of light danced through the closed curtains, revealing a fine spread of dust over the dark wood floors and the woodstove at the other end of the room. I cradled my rooting son closer to my chest as I settled on the couch and pulled up my shirt.

As I brought him to my breast, he refused to latch.

I used all the tactics and skills the nurses taught me: squeezing, flicking, football hold, cradle hold, hand-expressing, and switching sides. He clenched his fists and howled louder, and tears welled in my own eyes.

Daniel stopped in the doorway with our duffle bag in his hand. "What's wrong?"

"I can't get him to latch, Daniel," I said. My voice cracked. "What am I going to do?"

Daniel dropped the duffle bag on the threshold and shook his head. "Enough of this," he said. He walked past me and turned into the kitchen. He returned a few minutes later and dropped an unopened package of nipple shields[3] on the coffee table in front of me. "Here. Try these."

I frowned. "But what if they cause me to dry up? What if they ruin my connection with my baby?" I murmured. I had to breastfeed. I already chose an epidural, and that in itself felt like enough of a failure. How could I modify or even potentially lose breastfeeding as well? I gripped breastfeeding, entwining my goodness as a mother with it. To use a nipple shield made me a disappointment as a mother, especially if it ruined all hope of ever breastfeeding again.

---

[3] A nipple shield is a silicone device worn over your nipple to help your baby if they struggle with breastfeeding; it looks like a hat with a brim.

Daniel put a hand on my shoulder. "Lara, your baby can't latch and needs to eat one way or another. It's worth a try."

He squeezed me. "Besides, you have friends who use these and are completely fine. Just try, *please*."

I nodded. I gently pulled them from the packaging, read the instructions twice, and then put them on. As I lifted my son's head, he immediately latched and sucked greedily. I felt the milk fill me and empty into his tiny mouth.

"He's drinking, he's latching!" I cried. "How can it be so simple?"

Daniel laughed. "And we didn't even have to spend a week in the hospital."

We sat there, staring at our precious new boy, grateful for God's common grace.

As I beheld my suckling son, I realized that the story I had told myself about breastfeeding and holiness deafened the true gospel with my works. I put faith in my labors to sanctify both my children and myself. I trusted in something less than Christ's work.

We're both saved and sanctified by God's grace. God turned our hearts from stone to flesh by grace, and we still need that same grace to continue making our hearts into the likeness of Christ. Christ is our righteousness before God because we cannot earn a right standing before him. The Holy Spirit then sanctifies us towards holiness, even in motherhood. God will "equip [us] with everything good that [we] may do his will, working in us that which is pleasing in his sight, through Jesus Christ, to whom be glory forever and ever" (Heb. 13:21 ESV).

We can be tempted to put so much weight on breast milk—to the extent of calling it "liquid gold." But when we're done breastfeeding, where will we put that hope? Will we place it in school curriculums, healthy meals, or family devotions? Or will we place our hope in Christ? Christ is purifying *us* mothers into pure gold, and he can purify our children too. He saves *and* sanctifies us by the gospel (Phil. 2:12–13). Breastfeeding can't do that for us.

We don't have to utterly despair over our breastfeeding battles, but can take comfort in how Christ is transforming us and our children despite what we feed them.

The fall didn't surprise God, and neither did its effects. God knew sin would trickle down to us and make breastfeeding a thorn in our sides. But in his wise, good, and loving sovereignty, he likewise works it out for our good (Rom. 8:28–30). Perhaps these struggles we're having with breastfeeding right now are his way of refining us into purer gold. Maybe we will learn to persevere through difficulty by continuing to breastfeed or learn to trust God with our children's health as we feed them from a bottle. Maybe we will learn to be compassionate towards the mom who is giving her daughter formula.

We must guard against the boisterous sadness of breastfeeding difficulties that keep us from seeing God's hand weaving our stories. All suffering that we experience is being used to make us more like Christ. As Peter wrote to the persecuted Christians,

> In this you rejoice, though now for a little while, if necessary, you have been grieved by various trials, so that the tested genuineness of your faith—more precious than gold that perishes though it is tested by fire—may be found to result in praise and glory and honor at the revelation of Jesus Christ (1 Pet. 1:6–7 ESV).

Through whatever we're struggling we can all learn yet another way to preach the gospel to ourselves: Mourning what isn't right in the world, trusting in Christ for our salvation and sanctification, and rejoicing in the wholeness that is to come when we receive new bodies in eternal life. All the while, resting in our Savior, who hides us in himself and clothes us with his righteousness alone.

During my breastfeeding struggles, a nurse came regularly to check in and weigh my son. She arrived one day just as I sat down with my nursing pillow on the couch. She handed my gaping, rooting baby to me as I finished placing the shield on my breast.

She sat back in her chair, watching him nurse without a struggle. "Are you finding the shields helpful in your breastfeeding issues?"

I looked down at my boy, his eyes closed as he gulped and snorted like a little pig. "Yes, yes they are."

She nodded. "And are you happy to continue using them?"

I paused. I looked at her for a moment, searching her face to see if I could find the motive behind her question. Yet her brown eyes stared at me just the same, and the smile seemed unhindered. I looked down at my son again, where his hand clung to my pulled-up shirt. "Yes... Yes, I am."

4
An Identity Smothered in Diapers

As due by many titles I resign
My self to Thee, O God; first I was made
By Thee, and for Thee, and when I was decayed
Thy blood bought that, the which before was
Thine;
I am Thy son, made with Thy Self to shine,
Thy servant, whose pains Thou hast still repaid,
Thy sheep, Thy image, and, till I betrayed
My self, a temple of Thy Spirit divine

— John Donne, Holy Sonnet 2

Before becoming pregnant with my first son, my heart ached while I watched other women around me become pregnant. I saw the way their children hugged them and looked up at them and longed to have that as well. I saw them cuddling their newborn babies and craved to have my arms full as well. I gritted my teeth as I listened to them complain about their children or the pains of pregnancy. I wanted that—I wished I could groan with those complaints.

One day as I scrolled through Facebook, I saw a pregnancy announcement from a couple I went to school with. "They haven't even been married for a whole year!" I yelled from the couch.

A Mother Held

My husband and I weren't in a place to have children of our own, and I despised that lot God had drawn for us.

I wanted to be a mother because I wanted purpose. At the time, we lived in a cabin caged in by trees on a dirt road in the middle of Nowhere Land next to an abandoned church. While my husband worked all day, I sat in this tiny cabin, over an hour from any friends or family, with a fickle internet connection attempting to complete school work (though I knew that by next term I wouldn't be able to afford to even finish).

I not only felt purposeless—I felt like a scarecrow stuffed with hay and no identity.

Yet once I finally birthed that small child, motherhood ignored my plea to give me an identity—instead, it gulped my identity whole. I believed that when I first laid eyes on my new baby, my identity would explode like fireworks in my chest. Mothers talk about falling in love with their babies at first sight. Unlike when some met their husbands-to-be and falling in love was a process—love overtook them immediately. I believed that by feeling that immediate love I would find my identity.

During those long nights of nursing every two hours, wandering the creaky, moonlit halls with a baby who seemed to never stop crying, my cheeks and ears burned as I wondered, *Did I make a mistake? Was I ready? Is this the identity and purpose I longed for?* I thought of all the women with messy buns and babies on their hips, and the flat-lay pregnancy announcements that made me long for this moment. *This isn't what I thought motherhood would be.*

When we see motherhood on Instagram, we often scroll past cute boys and girls dressed in floral dresses and sweet suspenders. We see giggles and trim mothers carrying their infants in slings over their shoulders. We see the new smiling baby at church who falls asleep in the pew next to us. We think, "How much joy could motherhood bring me? How sweet would I look with a baby in my arms? How delightful would it be to see my baby smiling back at me?"

What we don't think about is the possibility that we may not always enjoy motherhood—that motherhood isn't all bliss and sloppy kisses. Or how we will cope when postpartum depression kicks in. Or how we will survive those endless days trapped in our home breastfeeding a baby going through a growth spurt. Or how we will make it through the colic.

I glared in the mirror while bouncing a baby with chronic acid reflux, only to see a haggard housekeeper with a screaming child pulling her hair. Sins I didn't know were so pervasive in my heart surfaced like dead fish in a pond. I rooted for my identity amidst the overflowing trash can of diapers, only to find it had been stolen.

In a way, I had grown into a modern-day Rachel, the wife of Jacob in the Bible, with my identity hunting.

As I read through Genesis, Rachel's words stung my own heart: "Give me children, or I will die!" she cried. She was fed up watching her sister birth baby after baby, meanwhile, her womb remained empty. It was enough of a burden to share her husband with her sister—now she had to watch her birth multiple children.

"Am I in the place of God," Jacob, her husband snapped at her, "who has withheld from you the fruit of the womb?"

She fought back tears and gritted her teeth. She had only one choice if she wanted children. "Here is my servant Bilhah," she said, "go into her, so that she may give birth on my behalf, that even I may have children through her." So she gave him her servant Bilhah as a wife, and Jacob slept with her.

If you've read the book of Genesis, this story may sound familiar. Genesis 30 recounts this story of Rachel's resolve to have children however she can. Rachel's life remained one marred by bitterness, discontent, and want. She had won the love of Jacob—he loved her more than her sister who he was deceived into marrying—but now she wanted children. Her sister bore children, but she did not.

A Mother Held

Rachel saw motherhood as her only source of joy, to the point that death was better than being childless. She became so desperate that she sold her husband to her sister for the night to get mandrakes (a plant she believed could strengthen her fertility) from her nephew. Historically, Rachel sat in a bit of a different place than most of us: She needed children to be honored and have a sense of pride because a child (particularly a boy) would carry on her husband's family line. Many social pressures and taboos encircled Rachel. She would be looked down upon, even though she was the one her husband first desired.

Though I didn't have the same extreme pressures as Rachel, I shared her fears. I needed to claim motherhood as my identity, otherwise, I had little to show for my life. I needed children to give me purpose and pride in my life. While I didn't fear rejection from my community as Rachel might have, I did fear their judgment of what I had to offer as a young, new wife.

Rachel and I put our hope and identity in motherhood rather than our Creator and Lord. Rather than trust in God who withholds no good thing (Ps. 84:11), we vainly sought to take our lives into her own hands. We constantly sought more, grappling and stretching, rather than resting in the love and grace of our Heavenly Father.

Finally, God gave Rachel the son she so desperately craved. But how did she respond? Many women who toil and grieve their infertility are often filled with joy when their first child is laid in the crook of their arms. Yet as she embraced this new life, she declared, "May the Lord add to me another son!" (Gen. 30:24). No gratitude, no worship to God for providing such a miracle—rather, *give me more*. We often believe the fulfillment of our longings will finally give us contentment, yet like Rachel, we catch ourselves with outstretched, wiggling fingers, demanding even more. That's where I sat, even after having my child: *This isn't the Instagram-worthy life I thought I'd have. People aren't exclaiming my greatness like I thought they would. I need something more.*

God beckons us to lay every burden at his feet and to lament our unfilled longings. Years later, another woman came crying to God over her lack of a child: Hannah. Hannah stood in a similar place as Rachel: one of two wives to her husband, infertile, watching the other wife bear children. Though not her sister, the other wife regularly mocked Hannah's childlessness. Hannah's husband seemed indifferent to her grievous longings; though he sought to show her extra affection because of her lack, he questioned her grief and her love for him because of it (1 Sam. 1:1–8).

One year as they worshiped God in Shiloh, Hannah journeyed to the temple. She wept before God and prayed for a child. She brought her agony to him, letting her grief pour out of her so much that the priest believed her to be drunk. But rather than holding tightly to that longing for a child, she promised to give her child to God to serve in his temple if he were to answer this one prayer.

I dwelled on both these stories while I bounced a child on my lap with my Bible and my eyes darkened from lack of sleep. While I did, I realized God laid before me two choices: to live as Rachel or Hannah. Though I never faced infertility, my two roads were the same: to idolize my children and raise my claws at God if he came too close to them, or fall on my face before him offering my child—and myself—to his will.

This truth doesn't change once we have those children we long for. Motherhood, I'm learning, consists of dying *of* self and dying *to* self, to the point that I don't always *recognize* myself. Motherhood changed me. At first, I believed it to be a crushing of myself, but rather I realized that caring for a child burned away the chaff in my heart and humbled me at the lavishness of God's love and grace. That hopeless state of lostness and sadness over the loss of myself came as I entangled my identity far too tightly in motherhood. I found my entire self in motherhood rather than looking at the true identity God sought to draw out:

A Mother Held

My life is hidden in Christ.

I am a woman made in the image of God, being transformed by the Holy Spirit into the likeness of Christ. I am the Father's daughter, receiving the inheritance for his children. I am a servant of the King. I am a mirror reflecting the glory of the Savior. I belong to Jesus as one bought by his righteous blood. I am only one piece of the body of the bride of Christ. I received undeserved grace. I am sinful yet righteous in Christ.

On those days of motherhood, when hot tears burned my eyes, my arms ached from carrying an infant, when I only had five minutes to myself because he cut his nap short, when writing and exercise got tossed in the back closet for later, this is where my hope and joy needed to be found.

Not in square pictures edited with the same filter and a child wearing trendy tan-colored clothes, but in my Savior who dwelled within and called me his beloved child.

One day I wandered into my bedroom with my first infant on my hip. A shower had not happened that day and naps were bismol. I wandered over to the mirror and caught a glimpse of us in the reflection: a mom whose frizzy hair hadn't seen a straightener for several days with spit-up stains on her clothes. She held a baby, covered in the same spit-up, still in his pyjamas. Both of our eyes looked exhausted because we were both in need of naps. A pile of dirty laundry overflowed from the basket in the background.

I snapped a picture with my phone of our reflection—to remember where we once were and look back one day to see how much we'd changed.

5
Memorial Pieces of My Home

> *What though sorrow seems to win,*
> *O'er hope, a heavy sway?*
> *Yet hope again elastic springs,*
> *Unconquered, though she fell;*
> *Still buoyant are her golden wings,*
> *Still strong to bear us well.*
> *Manfully, fearlessly,*
> *The day of trial bear,*
> *For gloriously, victoriously,*
> *Can courage quell despair!*
>
> — Charlotte Brontë, *Life*

Reminders of all I didn't have stalked me in my home. Four pairs of jeans hung in my closet with too wide of a waistband. I wore them during my first pregnancy before I had to finally give them up and buy some actual maternity jeans. I held onto them, expecting another pregnancy—yet they still lay unwrinkled with the edging of dust on the hangers as my womb recovered from miscarriage.

Each night I choked down a large prenatal vitamin to ensure I had all the proper nutrients just in case another baby burrowed into my womb.

A Mother Held

We painted our spare bedroom tangerine with a newly renovated bureau and an empty crib in the corner. Each roll of paint was a tug-of-war in my heart between trust and doubt as I wondered if this room would ever hold another baby.

An old wooden highchair became the scaffolding for spider webs in the basement, waiting to be refinished. I kept putting it off; I didn't need another memorial piece to remind me of what I may never have again.

Each of these pieces pricked at my heart like a sewing needle. They used to whack me like a mallet, but with time their blow had softened to an acute poke. They reminded me of my first—and still ongoing—season of grief. They remind me of the flickers between faith and unbelief that I bounced between in those early weeks of lament over our miscarriages.

We sat silently in the car, trees whirling by, nearly through our drive to the hospital in the darkness of night.

I recognized this scene all too well—the last several times we had made this kind of journey, they always ended in heartbeats and eventually a crying baby being birthed. Yet now, as I lay on the bed and a different doctor glided a probe over my womb, we heard no heartbeat and saw only an empty sac. His voice dully hit my ears as he discussed cramping, bleeding, when to return to the hospital, and the possibility of a D&C. I don't think I wept in the car. I only stared at the windshield as my body released its grip on our second child.

The next morning I rolled on my side as cramping seized my stomach. Tears streamed down my face, and I didn't want to go to the bathroom.

"It's over," I sobbed, hugging my pillow to my chest. "It's over." My husband stroked my hair and stood by my side until our only son cried out from his crib wanting breakfast.

When we had our first son over a year prior, I praised God for such a simple pregnancy and birth. There were minor complications here and there, the usual aches and pains and morning sickness. I became pregnant easily, birth came as naturally as possible, and we brought Levi home healthy and thriving.

I assumed because my first operated according to my timeline, the rest of my family could be ordered as simply as well. Yet in November, we lost this second baby within the first few weeks of her life in my womb.

That Sunday, I restrained and swallowed tears throughout the morning worship. I didn't dare lift my voice to sing, knowing what kind of sobs could wrench out. That afternoon, I sat in the sun by the open window in our living room. I felt like Job, demanding a court hearing with God. "What is God doing?" I whimpered. My Savior appeared like the cruel author of my story, scribbling out a tragedy for my life rather than one of redemption.

My husband gave no reply. A few minutes later, as the wind ruffled the linen curtain, our doorbell chimed. I wiped the tears from my face as I shuffled to the porch.

I was startled when I opened the door. The leader from my mom's group stood on my steps with an orchid and a steaming, foiled-covered meal in her other hand. She said she was so sorry to hear of our loss and she wanted to help us through this hard time. She had asked the other ladies of the group to cook a week's worth of meals for us.

After I thanked her, I stepped inside and slowly closed the door. I had no words.

The following week at the same mom's group, I kept my head down as I walked to my seat. I had bashfully announced my pregnancy weeks prior, and now I felt as if I had failed. My womb couldn't hold a baby; instead, it let it slip to its death. As I kicked my diaper bag under my chair, trying to hold onto numbness so tears didn't come, I felt a soft touch on my shoulder. I turned and looked into a pair of warm eyes. The woman pressed a plastic container of chocolate chip cookies to my chest with a card taped on the top. "I'm so sorry for your loss," she whispered. As she walked away, I peeled the card from the lid and read the inside.

I'm so sorry for your loss, dearest Lara. I know this secret grief as well. If you ever want to talk, I can be a listening ear.

I rolled my lips and blinked tears away.

As our Bible study time ended that morning, I gathered up my belongings and left the room to retrieve my son from the nursery. A woman I barely knew stopped me at the door as I passed the bathroom. "Hi Lara," she said. She had that sympathetic tilt to her head that most people adopted when they saw me. We exchanged the usual civilities, but when I thought she was done, her bright blue eyes locked on mine.

"I just wanted to say—" she bit her lip. "I just wanted to say... I'm so sorry for your loss." Tears brimmed in her eyes as she glanced over at her infant girl sound asleep in her car seat. "I'm sorry, I don't want to make you cry," she said, wiping the tears from her face. "I just can't imagine going through that. I'm so sorry."

My lip trembled. "Thank you."

A week later, I called the mom who gave me the cookies, and we met at my home. Sitting across from her while our little ones played on the floor, I told her my fears and heartache, and she bore them with me.

We chose to name this lost baby Kindness, as a reminder of a simple orchid, a hot meal, a small encouragement that showed me the lovingkindness of the Lord and that he had not left us as his children.

Upon the recommendation of a writing friend, I wrote Kindness a letter:

Dear Kindness—our second baby, our first miscarriage:

I remember when I first saw the word, "Pregnant," on the test, excitement flowered immediately at the thought of welcoming you into our lives. Tears of joy stung my eyes. I saw similar joy on your father's face when he found the test himself. Gratitude over your life filled us, so we set to work planning and preparing a place for you in our hearts and home. A few weeks later in the same bathroom, I was met with the joyful tears of learning about your life, tears rolled down my cheeks yet again—though this time because you were gone. I had only known you a handful of weeks, but I already loved you just as much as your older brother. I never imagined that I'd need to say goodbye so soon.

Losing you has been the foggiest valley I've walked through. I questioned if I would ever know daylight again. Sometimes I wondered if I would simply pitch a tent in this valley and never leave because I didn't know backwards from forwards. I miss you, Kindness, more deeply than I can express.

I find comfort in knowing you are in the hands of God. In his hands, you will never know pain, sorrow, or fear. In his hands, you will never experience unfaithfulness from another. In his hands, you are and will be perfectly safe and held. You will never cry, Kindness. And while I am so thankful for that for you, I selfishly wish that as frail as my arms are, they could have just one moment to cradle you.

I hope I never forget about you, and I will do my best not to. Yet I know my mind is weak, and for the times I do forget, God will remember you. I look forward to the day when we are reunited, as David said of his baby, "I shall go to him, but he will not return to me." One day you, Daddy, and I will meet again, and I pray that your older brother Levi will as well. But right now, God has other plans for us. We have to care for your brother and we have work to do. Until then, the Spirit encourages me that you are singing with the saints, "Holy, holy, holy, is the Lord God Almighty." I have to go back to caring for you brother, but as I do I will hold you in my mind and heart.

With all my love, *Mommy*[4]

While many women experience at least one miscarriage in their lives (one in four), they go on to create beautiful, flourishing families. People reassured me, "You'll get to be a mother again," or, "You'll have another one." While I knew better than to hold onto such false hopes, a part of me did.

---

[4] This is a letter I wrote to our first miscarried child during the week we lost her. This letter was modified for this book to help readers better understand its meaning and purpose.

Three months later, we rejoiced at the sight of another positive pregnancy test.

Despite how early it was, I planned again.

Fears of miscarriage tingled in the back of my mind, but I continued to reassure myself that I would go on to have as many healthy pregnancies as I wished. I planned the bedroom colors, the announcement, the to-do lists, the gender reveal, and even daydreamed about my son meeting his older brother in the hospital.

Yet a few days following the positive test, I began to miscarry again. We had no words or feelings, only numbness. We didn't know what to do or say, but we named this little one Jeremiah. Jeremiah means, "Yahweh will raise," and I wanted to be reminded that God would raise my baby to eternal life with us. The name Jeremiah likewise reminded me of God's words to this prophet: "Before I formed you in the womb *I knew you*" (Jer. 1:5 ESV, emphasis mine).

After this anguish and my collection of grief memorials, God opened my eyes to see another set of memorials he had laid out for me as markers of
his kindness.

In my office, a white frame sits on my bookshelf with a picture of hand-drawn mountains and rivers, all formed with words from Psalm 40. I look at it every day and remember God's loving kindness to his children.

For months a large glass baking dish sat on my back porch. It arrived in the arms of a friend nestled in oven mittens because the meal was still hot. It lay on the dryer for months, waiting to be carried out the door and brought back to its owner. Each time I passed the empty dish shouted at me of all the glimpses of Christ's love I saw through his church during our first *and* second miscarriages.

Around my neck hangs a gold chain with two tiny seeds encapsulated in the pendant. A gift from five long-distance friends reminds me of the two lives I carried for a short time in my womb and the love of the body of Christ that extends across countries.

And each night when I wrapped my husband's calloused hand in my own, I remembered his strong grip as I cried tears upon tears. The callouses reminded me of his steadfastness, of how much pain he walked through with me while never faltering in his love and care.

These memorials all pointed to one eternal truth: how God carries us through suffering at the hands of his people. With each loss, I looked up towards Heaven and asked God where his voice and his outstretched hand were as I collapsed under my grief. My eyes searched for the miraculous and supernatural, yet God continuously provided for me through the ordinary and natural and sought to direct my gaze to that providence through tangible memorials.

All of these items were memorials in my home, and Scripture itself even acted as an imperishable memorial. As I held my Bible each morning, felt the pages, and observed the curves of the words, their placement took root in my memory so that I could find them more easily each time I needed their comfort or reassurance. As I flitted through my house dusting and cleaning, I played the Bible in the background—suddenly places in my home became visual reminders of God's promises and acts of goodness. When I glimpsed the note cards with verses scribbled on them propped throughout my home, their exactness carved a spot in my mind. As I rewrote passages of Scripture by hand over and over, the phrases nestled in my heart. When I heard the Bible preached, it was as if God spoke directly to me.

God continued to fill my grief with little signposts to bolster my faith. From the small gifts from friends to the gathering of the saints on Sunday, my fragile heart was built up in the Lord. The singing of saints beside me, the preaching of the Word, and the holy memorials of communion and baptism. Tears rolled down my cheeks as I cheered for believers being washed in the waters and gripped the bread and wine in my hands. I beheld Christ's work he accomplished for me, for his people, and in that, I saw the supernatural my heart had longed for but didn't expect. In all of these memorials, Christ bent low for me.

The grievous memories remained and clung to their memorials, but God sought to continually turn my gaze back to the ones that proclaimed his faithfulness to us through them. The grief still knocked at our door on certain days and nudged my shoulder when I saw pregnancy announcements or heard others' stories of miscarriage. Even then, God carried me through and taught me how to hold on.

6
Grief and Joy In Tandem

"Hope" is the thing with feathers -
That perches in the soul -
And sings the tune without the words -
And never stops - at all -
And sweetest - in the Gale - is heard -
And sore must be the storm -
That could abash the little Bird
That kept so many warm -
I've heard it in the chillest land -
And on the strangest Sea -
Yet - never - in Extremity,
It asked a crumb - of me.

— Emily Dickinson, Hope Is The Thing With Feathers

The summer after my miscarriages, I watched resilient weeds push up through the sun-burnt grass on our lawn. Though the grass resembled fallen autumn leaves, the weeds stood tall with vibrant green stems and perky yellow and white petals. While our feet crunched over the grass on the way to the shore, tall shoots of Queen Anne's Lace tickled our calves. I couldn't help but wonder at these thriving weeds and wildflowers amidst all the withering grass and flowerbeds. Yet it seemed to be an adequate picture of the strange reality I'd felt as a believer residing in a fallen world.

A Mother Held

My husband and I still mourned two miscarriages. By this time I would have had a swollen stomach near delivery. As we lamented, we grappled with the whys—why two miscarriages and why at the moment when the season already felt so difficult?

By spring, I became pregnant for the fourth time, and we held our breath as each day passed in the first trimester. We finally received an assuring sign: morning sickness. But this morning sickness was unlike any I had experienced before; I woke up every day dry heaving and could hardly stomach the sight of food. Eventually, my husband had to take time off work while I crumpled into our bed for six weeks. Again, the *whys* crowded in—why, when we could finally celebrate life, must morning sickness utterly absorb any joy and rejoicing? Curled up on the bathroom floor I wept, "God, I can't do this. Please, please don't take this baby away, but please give me some kind of relief or hope to cling to."

One day, during a fit of uncontrollable dry heaving over the side of the tub, my husband called our doctor. I overheard the conversation—she told him to take me to the hospital.

"No!" I shrieked, clinging to the porcelain. "I don't want to go!" I wrenched out the words over gags and sobs. Yet we went anyway, knowing it was for the best. The nurses immediately hooked me up to an IV, ordered blood work, and wheeled me in a wheelchair to the ultrasound department. As I lay on the bed while the technician rolled the probe over my belly, I whispered, "I know the rules, but I've had two miscarriages. Can you at least tell me if there's a heartbeat?" I bit my cheek to hold the tears back. The technician kept her eyes on the screen, which she kept turned away from my sight. "I'm sorry, I can't. The doctor will be able to tell you soon."

Afterward, a nurse wheeled me back to my room where my husband eased me into the hospital bed. "Is the baby okay? Did they tell you anything?" he asked.

"No," I replied, letting a tear slide down my cheek.

We waited an hour before a doctor finally slipped in.

Lara d'Entremont

I imagine we looked at her like beggars in the desert, our eyes glued to her for some kind of real water to drink. A smile crept on her lips. "I have good news and... *interesting* news," she said. My arms twitched as if to reach out and grasp the hope she hid behind her clipboard. "You're pregnant... with twins."

My husband and I collapsed into each other's arms and wept. This was our hope amidst the crippling morning sickness, a salve to the nights of weeping and questions: Though we had lost two, God graciously gave us two.

While being the wonderful gifts they are, I knew those two baby boys wrestling in my womb would never replace the two we lost. I still shed tears when I think of my miscarried children, and I still wear my necklace with two seeds encased in the pendant as a reminder of their short lives.

When a joyous moment happens, many of us believe that all grief and heartache should instantly be erased. Like an incorrect answer to a math problem—we believe we can just brush away the shavings and continue with the right solution. But that's not the way grief works. A widow who remarried will never forget her first husband. A child's stepmother will never replace her biological mother who passed away. It's the same for parents of miscarried babies. No amount of children will replace the ones we lost. Grief and joy can be held in tension, two opposites somehow held together in a strange union. Tears of rejoicing and sorrow may mingle.

I'm reminded of Job. When Satan came before God requesting to test Job's faith, God allowed him. Job lost his children, much of his estate, and even his health. I wonder if he felt this tension of holding both grief and joy when God restored his fortune and gave him ten more children. Discussing Job's restoration, Sarah and Jeff Walton write, "Though I'm sure they rejoiced and loved their subsequent ten children, Job and his wife couldn't replace (or restore) the children they had lost.

Instead, they enjoyed what God had restored in their earthly life, while presumably still longing for the day when they would be reunited with their children in complete restoration."[5]

While living on this sin-cursed earth we will always be on a tight-rope walk of celebration and mourning. Some losses that caused us grief may be restored and replaced, while others will never be. In those times, we will walk our road holding hands with joy and grief, sometimes talking to one more than the other.

I felt this strangeness as my twin boys squirmed and kicked in my womb—while filling me with joy at the thought of cradling their wiggling bodies, I experienced deep grief for the ones I'll never hold. I remembered those wildflowers—something beautiful thriving among the withering of the parched grass. I marveled at the delicate loveliness of Queen Anne's Lace while my toes were scratched by burnt grass. At that moment, walking through the weeds, I sought to enjoy the goodness present within the lack. My husband and I rejoiced and celebrated those healthy babies flourishing in my womb without forgetting the ones who passed away before them. As we did, we looked forward to the expected rain of consummation to come—when the grass and wildflowers will both flourish unhindered, where death will be no more, where our hands will let go of grief and will continue down the path with arms linked only with joy.

---

[5] Jeff Walton and Sarah Walton, *Together Through the Storm* (Charlotte, NC: The Good Book Company, 2020), 273.

7
Longing for Home

Oh! when the heart is freshly bleeding,
How longs it for that time to be,
When, through the mist of years receding,
Its woes but live in reverie!
And it can dwell on moonlight glimmer,
On evening shade and loneliness;
And, while the sky grows dim and dimmer,
Feel no untold and strange distress—
Only a deeper impulse given
By lonely hour and darkened room,
To solemn thoughts that soar to heaven
Seeking a life and world to come.

— Charlotte Brontë, Evening Solace

Growing up, I don't remember having a comfort object. I didn't need a specific teddy bear to sleep, nor carry a special blanket over my shoulder. I didn't cry out for a certain doll to snuggle when I felt sick or scared. Rather, my security and comfort came from home itself—the winding stone paths through my mother's gardens, the green pond filled with frogs, the smells of cherry and apple blossoms mingled with horse hair and hay and the overbearing scent of evergreens.

This is where I knew I could escape from prying eyes and whispering voices to simply be alone and feel whatever I felt. Horses, barn cats, swallows, and chickadees wouldn't judge my tears of anxiety. I could also escape to my bathroom or bedroom without anyone hearing my panic over vomiting or crack open a favorite book to distract my obsessive thoughts.

This feeling has carried on from being a young girl to being a wife and mother. As a college student, it wasn't enough to be in the small living area of the dormitory pod I shared with my closest friends—I found true comfort in my room, the place where all my theologically sound books sat upon their shelves, the food I knew wouldn't upset my stomach was stowed away, and I could cry over the phone to my boyfriend without hearing the mocking voices of my friends.

Now as a young mom, a vacation or even a busy day in town makes me look forward to curling up on my couch. When I'm sick, I desperately long to be in the place I know best, even when the hospital tells me it's best to be in one of their beds. Though I've lived in many houses, whichever one we lived in at the time was my greatest security and refuge. Everything about the walls around me is a comfort to me—my bed, my couch, my blankets, my bathroom, my routine, my smells, and of course my family. All of what makes a place a home is my security blanket.

Yet being pregnant with twins, I had to consider the possibility that my babies might require time in the NICU—three hours away from where we lived. This thought frequently dredged anxiety up from my heart as I considered all that would mean. A 265-kilometer drive meant we'd be three hours away from our oldest son being cared for by his grandparents. Our first weeks as new parents could be spent in an unfamiliar hotel room, where I wouldn't recognize each scrape of missing paint on the walls, or the doors that don't close just right. How many nights would we go without goodnight kisses and hugs? How many days of takeout food and anxious waiting until we would finally share in the sights and smells of being together at our table again? All these questions and more haunted me as I awaited the day my babies came. I was homesick already, sitting in my living room.

Maybe you know similar feelings. Maybe you didn't have babies in the NICU, but instead, you were the one waiting in a hospital room wondering how many more days would pass before being released. You may feel homesick for old routines that your brand-new baby overturned. Or maybe you recently sold your house and moved away to a new city where you hardly know a soul. Maybe you feel homesick for the simplicity of life before babies.

Abraham likewise intimately understood what it was like to be uprooted from the place he'd always known:

> By faith Abraham obeyed when he was called to go out to a place that he was to receive as an inheritance. And he went out, not knowing where he was going. By faith he went to live in the land of promise, as in a foreign land, living in tents with Isaac and Jacob, heirs with him of the same promise. For he was looking forward to the city that has foundations, whose designer and builder is God. By faith, Sarah herself received power to conceive, even when she was past the age, since she considered him faithful who had promised. Therefore from one man, and him as good as dead, were born descendants as many as the stars of heaven and as many as the innumerable grains of sand by the seashore. (Heb. 11:8–12 ESV)

Abraham wasn't the only person longing for his abode. The author of Hebrews looked to Abel, killed by his brother Cain out of jealousy, who brought a pleasing offering to God. He wrote of Enoch, a man mentioned in a couple of sentences amid a family line, the one person whose account didn't end with "and then he died." Because of Enoch's faith, God took him to heaven without enduring the curse of death. The author of Hebrews goes on to write of Noah, who built the ark because water would fall from the sky—something he had never laid eyes on before—and would flood the earth to wipe out all mankind. By faith, God kept Noah and his family from being swept away and God preserved his line to Abraham.

> These all died in faith, not having received the things promised, but having seen them and greeted them from afar, and having acknowledged that they were strangers and exiles on the earth. For people who speak thus make it clear that they are seeking a homeland. If they had been thinking of that land from which they had gone out, they would have had opportunity to return. But as it is, they desire a better country, that is, a heavenly one. Therefore God is not ashamed to be called their God, for he has prepared for them a city. (Heb. 11:13–16 ESV)

Abraham was called by God to leave behind all that he knew. His family, his society's way of living, his false gods and their ways of worship, and the place where he laid his head each night to sleep. And by faith he obeyed. With this calling, God gave him a promise of a flourishing land and sons that outnumbered the grains of sand by the sea. By faith, he believed, though he was an old man with no children and spent his years living in tents.

Abraham died without beholding the fulfillment of this promise—only a glimpse of it in the birth of his son Isaac. How did he continue to believe God's Word? What kept him from turning around and going back to the land of his father?

By the persevering power of God, he kept his eyes not on the earthly aspect of the promise but the eternal one—the heavenly country, the city God had prepared for him. That's where his hope was found; the land where he would forever walk with God and be with God without the encumbrance of sin. The city where the ground was not cursed by sin, groaning for its release. We all want a safe, comforting place to call our familiar refuge. A place where we can curl up in a comfy chair with worn arms and sagging of the cushions that fit around us. A place where we can have messy hair and makeup-less faces without feeling self-conscious. A place where people who we love and who love us in return are eagerly awaiting our return. A place where we can cry and our tears won't make others feel awkward. A place where the people know our sins and love us still but strive to guide us toward holiness.

As believers, we all have this inheritance no matter where we are. We have this shelter in Christ.

It's the hope of this home that I strove to cling to, whatever happened when these beautiful babies came. Whether in hospitals, the NICU, hotels, doctors' offices, or in the comfort of my own house, I wanted to fix my eyes on the unchanging, perfect room kept for me in heaven. The one that will not tarnish, where all tears will be wiped away, where sickness will be eradicated, and where I will be with my Savior forever.

What makes heaven so lovely and should give us such hope isn't its golden streets and glowing rewards—rather, it's being with Christ himself. He is what makes heaven *heaven*—being unhindered in his presence without the lurking of sin. Though I love the roof over my head and find much earthly comfort in it, it is only temporary, and I am not a true citizen of it. My citizenship lies within the heavenly city where my Savior embraces me at the gates. That is my true home.

8

The Extra Hands and Feet I Need

Our created existence meant that from the beginning we needed the power of each other in order to live fully before God and enjoy his good world... Our creaturely bodily existence was designed for life-giving human relationships that occurred under the benediction of God.

— Kelly Kapic, Embodied Hope[6]

With the gift of twins, mornings initiated by dry heaving and nights on the bathroom floor barged in as well. At first, I tried to put my head down and grit through it, but eventually, I was forced to concede to my bed—for six weeks. Morning, afternoon, and evening blurred together as nausea dictated the bedroom lighting and sleep schedule. There were even a few trips to the hospital for dehydration. At one point I called my doctor to ask for more medication, and she told me, "I'm sorry, you're currently taking every anti-nausea medication."

During that time, I watched as each of my "backups" skittled to the ground. These backups were all the things I knew deep down

---

[6] Kelly Kapic, *Embodied Hope: A Theological Meditation on Pain and Suffering* (Downers Grove, IL: IVP Academic, 2017), 53.

that didn't make me right before God but gave me a false boost of confidence before him anyway. My clean home developed spots of mildew and crusted-on food. Laundry piled so high it required to be divided into two or three mounds. My robust, colorful meals became small and bland. My productivity nose-dived to zero as I lay in bed either half-conscious or watching Netflix. My mothering dwindled to a little more than a kiss before bed. My writing grew nonexistent. My daily Bible reading flickered away.

    I believed once the morning sickness ended and my children were born, I could place them under a schedule and I would return to my normal independence. Yet near the end of December, my obstetrician lifted my two little boys from my womb and nurses placed them against my cheeks, and I knew the lie I had believed. From the moment Daniel placed the tiniest one in my arms, I became keenly aware of my neediness as I took in their fragile bodies. With each feeding, each arm ache from carrying a fussy baby, each frustrated cry from my toddler who grew tired of hearing, "Please wait," and each interrupted nap on the couch, I felt a little more smothered by their needs.

    One day as I struggled to burp a baby while the other wiggled next to me, I muttered to my husband, "God should have given mothers of multiples the ability to grow an extra arm."

    During my entire pregnancy, I learned to bow my prideful, self-sufficient heart under God's fatherly hand. I spent the first six weeks in bed with crippling morning sickness while our parents cared for our toddler and cleaned our house. In the second trimester, I battled exhaustion and spent many afternoons at my mother-in-law's house so she could help care for our two-year-old. During the third trimester, I went into preterm labor and spent six weeks three hours away from my home under the care of a larger hospital, while our parents again took turns caring for our son around the clock.

Once our twin boys arrived, we had people in our home nearly every day helping us care for the twins, play with our little boy, and tend to housework.

I realized that this help was a gift, but at the same time, I began to despise my neediness.

I shared these feelings with my psychiatrist. "I'm ashamed of myself, that I need so much help," I told her. "I hear of other mothers of twins who are self-sufficient by six weeks. I'm embarrassed that I'm still asking for help every day. I should be able to do it on my own now."

She smiled at me. "So what if every mother in the world were self-sufficient at this point?" She went on to ask me if my well-being, which in turn makes me a better mother, is worth sacrificing so I can be self-sufficient.

"What if self-sufficiency isn't the goal?" she asked.

I don't know what my psychiatrist believed about God, but as I pondered her words I realized that Scripture is the origin of this idea: It is not good for man to be alone (Gen. 2:18). He made us in such a way that we need community and support.

As God humbled me before himself, he humbled me before my family as I had to renounce being their savior or hero. No matter how many scraped knees I kissed, how many meals I cooked, how many Bible stories I read, how many messes I tidied, how many life lessons I taught, how many hugs and words of comfort I gave, how much laundry I washed and folded, I had to come to terms with the truth that I will never be enough to sustain my family. As much as I desired to fix everything and protect my family from every possible trial, I was a creature and my Creator never created me to be that for them.

Rather, he formed each of us in his wisdom to need others. They need grandmas and grandpas and friends who are like family, along with their spiritual brothers and sisters from our church family. Countless meals were brought to our table by other people, our floors were swept by people who do not live here, dishes were washed by people who didn't dirty them, our laundry was cleaned and folded by people who did not own it. Many family members outside our household watched, fed, and played with my son. I received several texts a week asking how we were doing. Prayers were made by more people than I realized.

My family doesn't just need me—they need our community too. When the ocean waves roll towards me, God provides people to dig trenches around me and build rock walls to protect me, all the while God holds me up. But most of all they need their Savior to be their Solid Rock because I am about as sturdy as a sandcastle.

9
When My Body Failed

> *The soul is not an emanation of divinity entombed in a physical body; it is a natural but nonphysical aspect of our creatureliness. The soul is not divine, nor is the body demonic or evil; full humanity is a psychosomatic (body-soul) unity. We do not have a body (as if our soul were our real selves); we are created as a psychosomatic (soul-body) whole, as persons*
>
> — Michael Horton, Pilgrim Theology[7]

I cuddled my two-year-old toddler in the tiny space between the back of the couch and my swelling, 30-week belly. Daniel gathered up his lunch in the kitchen, then headed outside into the winter rain to stock the furnace with wood.

My boy babbled and shimmied out of his cozy spot on the couch. He crawled over my feet and grabbed a car to push along the coffee table, puttering with his lips for sound effects. I smiled at his boyish charm—until a sharp contraction seized my stomach.

I crumpled and cried out. My toes coiled together. My eyes squeezed shut. I breathed.

---

[7] Michael Horton, *Pilgrim Theology: Core Doctrines for Christian Disciples* (Grand Rapids, MI: Zondervan, 2013), 120.

Finally, it ended, and I relaxed back against the couch.

Until it came again.

"Ow!" I held my stomach and tears stung my eyes.

I breathed through my teeth as I wrestled my phone from under me.

Within a few rings, Daniel picked up.

"Hey?"

I swallowed, the pain finally easing. "Daniel, I'm having painful contractions."

"Call the hospital. I'm coming in."

He hung up and I quickly dialed the number. The receptionist transferred me immediately to the maternity ward.

"Good morning," a nurse answered.

I swallowed. "Hello, I'm Lara d'Entremont. I'm thirty weeks pregnant with twins and—" I gasped. A sharp pain hit me, and my whole stomach clenched tighter than any Braxton Hicks ever had. "I'm..." I sucked in through my teeth. "I'm having painful tightenings like contractions."

"It sounds like you're having one now," she said. "You should come in. How far away are you?"

"Thirty minutes."

"Okay. Leave now and we'll get ready for your arrival."

By that evening, the contractions had changed from irregular to a predictable pattern and I had a bloody show. After that internal check, a young, sweaty doctor looked at me and said, "I'm calling the IWK. You'll be flown to Halifax."

Within a couple of hours, my husband had already dropped off our son at my in-laws' house and left to begin his three-hour drive by car. Meanwhile, nurses strapped me to a gurney, rolled me into an ambulance, drove me to an emergency airport, and airlifted me to another hospital. A nurse fought all night to stop my labor—and successfully did. We breathed a sigh of relief, believing all difficulty was over.

A Mother Held

As I sat in the maternity ward of the new hospital, I settled back in bed with Daniel by my side.

A nurse entered and I casually asked her, "So when do we get to go home?"

She looked between my husband and me. "Has no one told you yet?"

I shrugged my shoulders. "No, we've been pretty in the dark."

She looked down at her white sneakers. "Oh gee, I hate it when they do this." She looked out at the large window, taking in the city lights against the blackness. "Alright, I hate to be the bearer of bad news, but here it is: Since your home hospital isn't equipped to deal with preemies, you'll have to stay here until you reach full-term."

My breath caught in my throat. My stomach felt as if it held a bowling ball. "What? How... how long is that?"

"Until you reach thirty-seven weeks."

A black hole seemed to open under me in the bed sheets, hurtling me through the darkness.

Seven weeks from home.

Seven weeks in a small room with no loved ones or friends.

Seven weeks away from my beloved two-year-old.

All because my body failed to hold my children safely inside on its own and decided to try to push my babies out too early.

Snow tumbled from the sky as I paced the living room floors. Our toddler slept in his bed and my husband eyed me nervously. I was thirty-seven weeks pregnant, only three days home from the city. Contractions had been coming and going all morning—but they seemed minor and inconsistent.

"Lara, I think we should go in," Daniel said, running a hand through his hair. "Can I please call my mom to come watch Levi?"

I grimaced as a contraction came and slowly dissipated. "No," I said, "It's probably nothing."

He exhaled loudly. "I don't want you to go into labor here, and I don't want to drive in a snowstorm. Please, can we go?"

I finally agreed, and we went to the hospital. Eventually, the contractions became regular—but something wasn't right. I sat in a labor and delivery room gritting against contractions and watching a monitor to see if my baby's heart rate would drop dangerously low for the third time. I lay on a hospital bed with wires, cords, and tubes connected to me everywhere. A nurse bent over me holding one of two dopplers at a twenty-five-degree angle on the underside of my swollen belly so we didn't lose Baby A's heart rate.

"Baby B's heart rate keeps going down whenever she has a contraction," a nurse said to my obstetrician.

The obstetrician looked between us. "If his heart rate drops three more times, I'm highly recommending an emergency c-section."

Everyone in the room watched the monitor without speaking as the next three contractions came over me. Drop one. Drop two... Drop three.

"Lara, do I have your consent to do an emergency c-section?" the OB asked.

Tears spilled over my cheeks. "Yes," I sobbed.

Within the hour, nurses rushed me to the operating room for an emergency C-section. We welcomed our twin boys into the world seven days before Christmas. After five long days in the hospital filled with weighings, bloodwork, IVs, and blood sugar checks, we were finally released with the ominous words, "Your family doctor must weigh them every few days. If they aren't gaining weight, you *must* come back. And we might need to do feeding tubes." I drove home in tears. I tried to enjoy our first Christmas with our twin boys, but I felt suffocated under numbers, breastfeeding, pumping, bottling, and sleeplessness as I crept through our house, bent at the waist, holding my healing incision.

A Mother Held

In the following weeks, my body continued to fail me. In an attempt to protect my children and me from harm, my mind hit "replay" on each memory and drew me back to the operating room. My broken mind sought to use flashbacks to remind me of the place where one of my babies nearly died and when my body didn't do what it was supposed to so that I'd never return to that dangerous place. Whenever I tried to share my birth story, sweat beaded on my neck and my throat tightened with panic (and still does most times). Nightmares of birth and another pregnancy haunted me like ghosts.

Some days I look at my body and think of it as a prison to my soul. My soul is good, but my body is bad; my soul is my truer self, while my body is a rusty cage from which I'm waiting to break free. It has stretch marks, it restricts me, it embarrasses me, it deceives me, it makes me sick, and it causes me sorrow. Sometimes I think of my body as an old car that isn't worth putting money towards fixing anymore. It doesn't seem to do much good anyway. I often become frustrated with my body and the way it looks and limits me, especially in motherhood: miscarriages, c-sections, exhaustion, morning sickness, and a host of mental ailments.

We're each covered in scars of some sort—whether from the scalpel of a doctor or emotional trauma inflicted on us—because of a greater scar that mars creation. When Adam and Eve disobeyed God, they not only passed down sin to their children but the brokenness caused by sin. Because of sin, all of creation isn't functioning as it should. Rather than strumming out perfect chords, there's a snapped string and a few are out of tune. This means that babies are born premature, some babies die, and some wombs refuse to grow little ones. This brokenness is seen in our painful travails, our aching bones, our weeping, and every sickness or impairment we carry.

Our bodies don't function as they should. My womb should

have cradled babies, but it allowed two to be lost before my twins. My body should have cradled my babies until they reached full term, but failed to do so. My body should have started labor on its own, but instead, I had to be induced. My twins should have been able to handle the pressure of birth without becoming too stressed out, but one of them did. My mothering mind should have felt only love and the desire to nurture, but it misfired and caused panic, flashbacks, and sadness instead.

I know I'm not the only mother feeling the ache of creation that Paul wrote about: "For we know that the whole creation has been groaning together in the pains of childbirth until now. And not only the creation, but we, who have the firstfruits of the Spirit, groan inwardly as we wait eagerly for adoption as sons, the redemption of our bodies" (Rom. 8:22–23 ESV). We groan, and all creation groans, because of the scars of sin. While our broken bodies are not a punishment for our sins or sins in themselves, they are a result of the curse of sin brought upon all creation when Adam disobeyed God.

Yet our greater hope is that one day all will be restored in heaven. Our grief and pain will be wiped away with perfect love found in being present with our Father and Savior. All will sing in harmony again. But until then, we live in this broken world listening to it sing out of tune.

Thank God that isn't the full story.

When Adam and Eve received the curse, they also received a promise: that all will be redeemed for those who trust in the serpent-crushing Son. Though he will be struck on his heel on our behalf, he will save his people from the curse and their sins. After rising from the dead, he promised to return for his beloved bride and bring her to the banquet feast and the home he has prepared for her, where her every ailment, tear, and grief will be washed away by his mighty hand.

For the in-between, God doesn't leave us as orphans. My body accomplished a great feat. It grew and sustained two babies together in the same womb. It was opened up and healed back together, leaving only a scar behind. It endured hormone fluctuations. It experienced physical and emotional trauma. Though in some ways it faltered, in many other ways it did something breathtaking. This doesn't just testify about the greatness of the female body; this testifies of our great Creator who made it all, designed it all, and sustains it all. This God, in his grace, provided a way in our broken world.

In the Fall, both the soul and body were broken by sin. Our bodies were then plagued by sicknesses and diseases, and ultimately death. Our bodies would be pushed and worked hard to survive. What was created to live with God in a perfect relationship forever would now return to the dust it came from—but not without enduring physical hardships.

But before this, when God formed us, he declared the whole of us as good—not just the soul. Both are created by God, both are created to glorify him, and both will be redeemed by God.

Yes, my body failed, just as each of our bodies fail in one way or another. But we worship Jehovah-Jireh—the God who provides and calls my body very good. My scars are not a testament of shame or proof of why I should hate my body but of the realness of God. The God who heard my cries as hormones caused my brain to misfire and provided relief through secular therapy. The God who carried my faith as I walked doubled over while holding my stitches. The God who was near when my womb couldn't hold the two babies before our twins. The God who never let me go when my body struggled and my faith struggled even more. Sometimes he provided physically—with medications that halted labor and a surgeon's scalpel. But he always provided himself—in all his fullness, in all his grace, in all his gentleness, and in all his love.

10
Watching Deer

For as I walk the wooded land
The morning of God's mercy,
Beyond the work of mortal hands,
Seen by more than I see,
The quiet deer look up and wait,
Held still in quick of grace.
And I wait, stop footstep and thought.
We stand here face to face.

— Wendel Berry[8]

Everyone wanted to know the story of how my twin boys were born at the same time.

"Tell me your birth story! I'd love to hear!"

I'd smile. I'd be polite. Each time I believed it would go differently, but it never did. I'd start telling the story, then the sweat dampened me like dew. Invisible wires tightened around my chest, cutting off my breathing. Words would disappear from my mind as I grappled to explain. My mouth would dry as tears formed in my eyes.

I'd finish the story and gulp water from my bottle. The friend or family member would nod and exclaim how wonderful it was that I had healthy babies.

---

[8] Wendell Berry, *A Timbered Choir* (Berkeley, CA: Counterpoint Press, 1998), 26.

A Mother Held

    I don't think anyone ever noticed me trying to catch my breath afterward. One of the ways I recovered was by watching out the window. Ever since moving into this home four and a half years ago, deer have traveled through our yard. This year, with my four-year-old and my twin toddlers watching next to me, a family of three deer travel and linger in our yard—a mom and twin fawns. When we catch them in our field, we pause whatever we're doing and stand at the door or window to watch them graze and play. The fawns often run and kick at each other, their white tails high in the air. After a while, the mother ambles into the woods and calls for her babes to follow her. Sometimes one will linger, or try to incite his sibling to go for one last kick across the lawn. But they always trail after her not long afterward. I don't think I've ever wondered about how that gentle doe birthed her twin fawns. Maybe we have an understanding between the two of us.

    I've always wanted to watch them nurse, but I've never caught sight of that yet. I think it would come more naturally than my experience ever did. Right after birth, we woke our newborn boys to breastfeed, pump, and then supplement with a bottle every two hours. Once we got them back to sleep, we had to clean the breast pump gear. One had low blood sugar, the other jaundice. One was a little under normal weight, the other quite underweight. They were three weeks early. Somehow, in all of this, I was supposed to shower, eat, sleep, walk, rest, and be self-sufficient to prove we were ready to go home.

    One evening while we were still in the hospital, as we finished cycling through the feeding process, I finally laid back in my hospital bed to close my eyes to sleep.

    Seconds later, I flung my eyes open and jolted up. My heart raced. Sweat broke out on my forehead and neck. My limbs felt weak.

    I tried to close my eyes. But the image gripped me again. And again. And again.

    In tears, I asked my husband to call one of the nurses in. She came and sat on the edge of my bed, a hand on my blanket-covered knee. I tried to tell her what was happening, but my sobs kept me from speaking clearly.

"Every time I try to sleep, I—I—" I cried.

"You can't turn off your mind? You can't relax? The babies' little noises keep you awake?" she asked.

Those were all normal experiences I had heard from others. I expected those; I knew they were normal. But no one prepared me for what was happening to me now.

"No," I said, rubbing my eyes. "Every time I close my eyes, I'm on the operating table again and my baby's heart rate keeps dropping."

That sweet mother fawn never experienced any of that. I bet sleep and feeding her babies came so simply to her. But the other night, one of the fawns darted across our front lawn. We had friends over, so I called them to the window to come see him. We all stood at the window at the exact moment when a truck drove by over the speed limit and hit the baby deer without ever slowing down. We live on a straight stretch of road, so people like to treat it like a race track. That night was a prime example of it, only this time a creature was harmed by someone else's heedlessness and irresponsibility.

I didn't know if I wanted to cry or scream, be angry or sad. The fawn tripped into the bushes and disappeared. We discussed what we should do, but it seemed that hope had to be lost—even if we did find this fawn in the bushes, was there anything we could do for him?

My husband and one of our guests went out to find the fawn while the rest of us watched from the window. As Daniel waded through the brush and bramble, someone said, "I see the ferns moving over there." We all cried out as a little white tail bounced out of sight away from Daniel.

We didn't see the fawn again that night, so we weren't sure if he limped away to die somewhere else or if he had recovered and found his family again. We tried to have hope.

A Mother Held

I watched the bushes as my heart squeezed together. Will she remember this? Will the memories seem to grab her out of nowhere, like they do for me? I could be holding my littlest son, and the shaven spot on his head where the IV had been would drag me into the low-lit rooms of the hospital. A Christmas song in our van proclaiming Christ's birth would haul me spiraling into the bright lights of the operating room. Will she face these memories now every time she must cross the road?

One day as I sat on my couch trying to balance two infants at my chest, I scrolled through the posts on a motherhood psychology Instagram account. I came across a post about birth trauma. As I read through the symptoms, I recognized each in myself—the flashbacks, the rage, the intrusive thoughts, the nightmares, and the jumpiness. I swiped out of the app and put my phone down to burp one of my babies. That couldn't be me though.

My experience wasn't traumatic enough. I had a safe birth, and my babies were both healthy and thriving. Even if I was experiencing birth trauma, I could never tell anyone. This wasn't normal, and I was a pathetic weakling if a mere C-section with kind doctors and nurses invoked a trauma response within. No one could know.

If that mother doe experiences this kind of trauma, she'd be justified in it. If she woke up in the night needing to reassure herself of everyone's safety, I wouldn't doubt her.

I regularly sprung up to a sitting position, gasping, in the middle of the night. The room would be dark, except for the stream of moonlight from outside. I'd blink and look around, taking note of the feel of the soft blankets gripped in my hands.

I'm in my bed. I'm home. My little ones are sleeping, safe and sound. They are healthy, we are okay. That's what I'd tell myself.

This kind of nightmare hasn't happened for a while. It seems they're growing more and more spaced apart, just as my psychiatrist said they would.

"I feel ashamed," I had told her. "My birth wasn't that traumatic. Why am I responding like this?"

"It's not about what happened, but how your body perceived it," she told me. "You are made to protect those babies. It's instinct. You're also made to stay alive. Your body perceived a threat to not only your life but your babies' lives, and so to protect you all from further danger, it's creating all these reminders and warning signals. You're not making yourself respond this way; it's simply nature."

"Will it ever get better?" I asked.

She nodded. "With time. As your body is shown and reminded that everyone is safe and all is well."

I watched for those reminders, and that mother deer gave me one.

The morning after the truck hit the fawn, I sat at my desk in front of the office window. A bit of movement caught my attention, so I looked up and saw the mother deer. She stood elegant and calm, head bowed as she chewed on grass. I stopped clattering on the keyboard and watched the bushes where she had come from. One baby deer wandered up the hill. I frowned as I watched him roam the yard alone.

She lost one of the twins—like I nearly lost one of my twins.

Not wanting to dwell on whether animals felt grief or not, I started to sit down to resume my writing, but something caught my eye. I looked up again and saw the other fawn walk up behind his brother. They kicked and sauntered through the field as their mother patiently waited by the forest's edge. Finally, they disappeared together into the woods.

They made it. They're safe. I listened to my little ones watching a cartoon in the kitchen behind me, slurping milk and crunching crackers.

My little ones are making it too, and my heart is beginning to feel a little bit more at peace.

11
What If It's Me?

Grant that I may always lift up unto you holy hands, without fear or doubt, and in full assurance that all my prayers and sighs which come from the heart, are truly heard. Grant also that when my help delays I shall be patient, not dictating to you either time or measure, but to wait and abide your own good time; for you have pleasure in them that fear and put their trust in your mercy.

— William Loehe[9]

Anxiety shows up like this:

I'm suffocated.
I jolt.
I pace.
I hum in a shrill voice.

In this story from my childhood, every muscle coiled up like a spring. I curled up in a red wingback chair in my parent's house reading a novel, digging my toes into the rough fabric. I was elementary-school-aged. My mom sat perched forward watching a crime show while my father was in the barn feeding the horses for the night.

---

[9] William Loehe, "Day 11," Prayer of Intercession in *Be Thou My Vision: A Liturgy for Daily Worship*, ed. Jonathan Gibson, First edition (Wheaton, IL: Crossway, 2021), 105.

I stared at the pages in front of me, but the words wouldn't penetrate my mind. Four words clenched my brain instead: Blaspheme the Holy Spirit.

A few weeks prior, I read about the unpardonable sin in my Bible. As I tried to force myself to focus on the pages of my novel, the phrase, "Blaspheme the Holy Spirit!" resounded on repeat in my head.

As a little girl, I lived in terror of my Heavenly Father abandoning me or casting me away. In my mind, he put up with me because he had to and waited for a moment he could justify throwing me out of his family. That's the way my earthly father looked at me—why wouldn't God look at me that way as well?

Meanwhile hellfire and brimstone ignited panic in my soul. I saw lava and people I loved screaming for help but unheard. I never wanted to go there. Despite believing God didn't want me, I couldn't leave him either and suffer the consequences.

I clutched my book harder, squeezed my eyes shut, and shook my head, trying to will the thoughts away. *No, no, I don't want to!* I cried silently. *I don't want to go to hell!* Yet the phrase repeated over and over again, seemingly louder each time. Heat electrified my body from my toes to my head while pins and needles raced behind it. My heart thumped in my chest.

"I'm going for a walk outside," I blurted, jumping up from my chair.

"Okay," my mother responded. To my relief, she hadn't noticed my panic.

Mist clung to the air, and the droplets cooled my body. Weaving through my usual path distracted my brain to let go of the repetitive thoughts. I did my usual turn through the trails, over the handmade bridge, along the riverbanks and ponds. I took note of the plants and wildlife and jumped over puddles and along the rocks that lined the water.

The beauties of nature distracted my mind from its obsessive thoughts, and I allowed myself to be drawn into my latest story idea as I walked.

I imagined myself a powerful heroine, able to conquer any beast or person that came for her. She always had a knight in shining armor of sorts—someone who loved her unconditionally, who promised to never leave her, and who always remained faithful. My heroines were always who I wanted to be and already had the things I longed for.

I returned inside to begin my bedtime routine: brush my teeth; check the shower and bathroom cupboard for monsters, ghouls, or kidnappers; knock the creepy doll's head down; pray the same prayer to protect everyone I knew; climb into bed.

While I lay in bed that night, the thoughts drifted back. I fought against them, but the hot fear rose inside me again. *What if God can no longer love me? What if God has cast me out?* Tears welled in my eyes as I thought of the fires of hell described in the Bible, the complete separation from God's love.

As the words pulsated in my brain, I thought of the late-night youth group conversations about demons. What if a demon caused this? I curled up tighter under the pink sheets, pulling my feet underneath myself. Shapes formed in the darkness of my room. I leapt from my bed and flicked on my bedroom light, then jumped back into bed just as quickly, my entire body shaking.

The thoughts kept coming.

I buried my face in the pillow. *Go away, go away, go away!* I knew I couldn't tell anyone what I experienced. If they knew I was permanently cast out of God's love, they too would cast me away. Or if they thought a demon haunted me, they might fear coming too close. I fought and resisted until my young mind could fight no longer and eventually tired out, where nightmares played all night long.

I jolted from the bed, sweat slick on my back. I was twenty-one years old and the mom to my first child.

"Daniel, Daniel!" I whispered, shaking his shoulder.

He groaned and blinked, then jumped as my voice pitched. "What? What's wrong?"

"Levi," I whispered. "What if... What if someone stole him? Someone could break into the house, and his room is the closest one to the door. They'll go there and we won't even know. We should do something... maybe we should lock or barricade his door... but then what if there's a fire..." My heart slammed in my chest like a mallet to a nail.

Daniel blinked and shook his head. "Lara, that's not going to happen. The door is locked."

My heart continued to hammer. "What if they go through the window?" I whispered. Tears pooled in my eyes. "I don't think I locked it." I gripped his shoulder. "Please, please go check."

Daniel stared at me with his mouth hanging open. He blinked sleepily, then nodded. "Alright."

A new ritual hooked into my mind: Check all doors and windows several times before going to sleep. Yet even then, thoughts and nightmares assailed me of someone kidnapping my child—or worse.

I paced the hallway with my sleeping infant. I tried laying him down in his crib several times, but each time he woke up screaming. He finally passed out in my arms while pacing the hallways, and I didn't dare set him down. I eased his floppy head onto my shoulder and tiptoed to the laundry room. The laundry could be thrown into the dryer with one arm, right?

As I eased my left arm from his bottom to not wake him, an image flashed across my mind. Behind my closed eyelids, I saw the baby slip from my arms and drown in the washer.

I gasped and jumped back from the washer, gripping him even tighter. I vowed to never bring him to the laundry room again.

I whirled around the kitchen—a hurricane of tidied-up dishes, toys, and spit-up rags. Early in marriage, I assigned kitchen chores to Monday, so the entire room had to be completely clean by bedtime—but within the proper order of the weekly checklist, of course. Who knew what kind of chaos could erupt if I broke this pattern? I'd be an unfit mother, an unloving wife, and a lazy homekeeper.

As usual, I had a half-asleep baby in my free arm, barely peeking around with his big brown eyes. As I turned around the corner, an image halted my steps: My infant's head smashing into the corner of the wall. Blood everywhere. Repeat, repeat, repeat.

Sweat pricked the back of my neck. I sucked in a breath between my teeth and gripped my child's soft head.

What if the danger isn't someone breaking in—what if it's me?

Violent images and thoughts assailed my mind like darts every day. I gritted my teeth as my stomach roiled. I stopped bathing my children and assigned the task to my husband—all I could see was their deaths in the suds. Whenever I pulled a shirt over their heads, I feared suffocating them. Blankets and straps looked like weapons. I checked on them periodically while they slept, to make sure they were still breathing, despite how weary and overwhelmed this task was amidst all the other work I had to do.

Yet each day, I smiled for family and friends and told them how wonderful motherhood was—what other option did I have? If anyone knew what was going on in my head, they'd take my children away. How can a good mother have such violent thoughts on repeat in her mind about her children?

I closed the door to my bedroom and logged into my virtual meeting with my psychiatrist. She asked the routine questions about my meds, sleep, and mood. But then she asked a question that caused sweat to bead on my forehead.

"Do you have any intrusive thoughts?"

I felt heat rise to my face. "What do you mean?"

She described an intrusive thought and gave examples. Violent, sexual, or religious thoughts popping into your head out of nowhere... persistent and difficult to control... causing anxiety and distress...

Heat tingled through my body, and sweat dripped down my neck. My heart pounded. My stomach churned. *I must lie.* I believed that if she knew the truth of what lurked in my brain, she'd sentence me to be hospitalized and take my children away in one fell swoop.

She finished her descriptions and definitions and then tucked a strand of hair behind her ear. "They are completely normal. We're unsure why mothers have them, but they do. They're upsetting but completely harmless. What makes them distressing is that they're the exact opposite of what you want to do. It's just your brain misfiring."

Just as the panic had risen inside me, a cool wave washed it away with her words. I repeated her words in my mind. *Normal.*

The opposite of what I want to do. Tears stung my eyes. "You won't take my children away if I have them?"

She waved her hand. "Of course not. They are completely normal."

I explained the thoughts that flashed through my mind and she simply nodded understandingly. "Yes, all very normal." She wrote something down and looked up at me. "Is this something you've struggled with before having children?"

I chewed my lip and thought. Memories came flooding back from my childhood: *Blaspheme the Holy Spirit... rituals... repetitions... violent images... scenes from movies repeating in my mind...*

I snapped back to the present. Slowly, I nodded. "Yes... Yes, I think this has been going on for a long time."

My psychiatrist nodded sympathetically and poised her pen over her desk. "Tell me what you remember."

I told her memory after memory from my childhood, teenage years, early months of marriage, and from my pregnancies and post-partum experiences; the memories seemed to pour out from a shattered bottle and run into channels as we both began to make connections.

She nodded. "Yes, I would say you have Obsessive-compulsive Disorder."

"Okay." I felt like hot and cold water flushed through me.

After my appointment, I joined my husband and children outside in the soft afternoon light, where shadows stretched from the swingset like gangly arms and legs. He shaded his eyes and smiled at me. "How'd the appointment go?"

I shrugged. "Fine." I swallowed. "I guess I have OCD." I looked off at the twins collecting pebbles. "I suppose it explains a lot."

My husband nodded. "How do you feel about it?"

I looked down. "Like I'm broken."

He closed the space between us. "I'm sorry." He lowered his head, trying to find my eyes. "But you know you're still the same Lara I love, right? You're still the same."

I smiled a little. "Thank you."

My diagnosis, my thoughts, and my compulsive actions didn't drive Daniel away. They drew him near—in my infirmities, he sought to be as much of a rock and shield as he could be for me to cling to keep my head above water as thoughts assailed me like arrows. He drew near—he never ran away.

12

The Purpose of My Home

> *I want to be a Christ for my neighbor, as Christ has been for me. I want to do nothing other than that which I see my neighbor needs, what is useful for him and is a blessing for him, because I have in Christ all that is sufficient for me through faith.*
>
> — Martin Luther, On the Freedom of the Christian[10]

A superhero raised me. Perhaps my mother would even put Superwoman to shame. She worked hard-labor jobs—fish plants, housekeeping, and food service. Yet as she toiled over these full-time jobs, she washed my clothes the same day I wore them. I got off the bus each day to a house smelling of boiled vegetables and roasted meat. She drove me to youth groups, piano lessons, skating lessons, and friends' houses, arriving early to both drop me off and pick me up. She made the beds each day without a single wrinkle and packed the perfectly balanced lunchbox. Dust and cobwebs didn't stand a chance in our house.

I learned that a superwoman doesn't always produce superhero offspring—but the urge to master my home with inhuman strength became my obsession.

---

[10] Martin Luther, The Freedom of a Christian: A New Translation, trans. Robert Kolb, of Crossway Short Classics (Wheaton, IL: Crossway, 2023), 77–78.

Before I became pregnant, I already committed to myself and Daniel that I would not let my housework fall apart simply because we had children. I set my face like a stone and aspired to keep the same high standards my mother did.

A few weeks into pregnancy, my kryptonite emerged as morning sickness and nausea consumed me. I strived to push through, to bear up with shields under the jaws of it. Yet within a week, I found myself curled up on the couch for hours at a time. Sickness became an endless, dark tunnel with no light up ahead. The few times I grasped relief, my body gave way to sleep.

I let exercise go unchecked in my planner, sent texts to cancel babysitting jobs, and watched laundry pile up in the corner of the bedroom and bathroom. Most days I pulled myself from the couch cushions to attempt meal prep, but I often dropped my knife after gagging over the smells of raw carrots and potatoes. I kept the living room curtains closed because the sunlight revealed a layer of wood scraps, dog hair, and dust covering our floors.

One afternoon, after a three-hour nap, I woke up not rested but ashamed and anxious. I resented how pregnancy debunked all my routines and tattered my tidiness. Though Daniel never seemed bothered, I cried and apologized daily for the messy floors and my excess sleep. I knew I needed rest, but the amount my body demanded overwhelmed me. I wanted to force myself into my old routines, but my body refused. Daniel attempted to pick up the slack, which only caused more bitterness for my lack of ability.

More than that, it triggered an itchy anxiety in me as I saw those tiny tumbleweeds of dog hair and the shirts not hanging in the correct order. I tried to ignore them, to pass them by, knowing I had no strength to tend to them. But like a rash, I couldn't ignore them—so I crawled on my hands and knees collecting tufts of dust and hair.

Well-meaning books, podcasts, and articles suggested that my grief and distress over desiring a perfectly clean home had become an idol in my life; they suggested I had allowed my desires to take hold of my heart and capture the throne. Those words pierced me with further shame. I desired to love God with all my heart, yet no matter what I did, I couldn't stop my obsession. Even the pain of the pregnancy was dwarfed by the need to clean.

Friends tried to encourage me and lift me from my angst by reminding me I wasn't superwoman. Yet it made no difference whether or not I was capable of upholding my standards—I had to return the order to my home and defeat the dust bunnies, even if it ruined me.

Once the twins were born, I vowed to reclaim control. Morning sickness had crippled me for a time, but I refused to remain in that place of inability to keep up with my housework, not even once they left my womb. I could be a superhero too; I simply had to work harder, grit my teeth, and press on. I spread my cleaning routine over Monday to Friday to make keeping up with housework possible. I assigned certain rooms to each day: Mondays for the kitchen, Tuesdays for the living room, and so on. It felt more doable than cramming all the chores into one day. Along with this schedule, I made a rule for myself in the name of conserving energy: if part of the list for each day didn't get finished, it wouldn't carry over to the next.

I walked through other people's homes and marveled at their dustless decor, shiny floors, and dinner tables without food stuck on them. How did they do it? How did they keep up so well? I sought to immerse myself in the conversations and meals happening around me, but my mind mentally compared my little home to theirs. I longed to return the favor of inviting them back into my own home, yet shame screamed in my ear that such a moment would be the ruin of my life. I'd never recover from such humiliation.

 Fine, I told the shame. *I'll break my back making sure it's sparkling before any guests walk through my doorway.*

 But sweeping five minutes before friends and family arrive doesn't stop the dog from scratching her ears and sending poofs of fur into the air, or the stain I can't get off the floor, or the way the ten-year-old wallpaper plastered in the closet is slightly ripped. Shame always found something to snarl about as I served our guests, like how the spindle on our old chair had a crack in it and the paint was chipped. Every evening as I closed the door and waved to those driving away, I returned to my living room to stew about all the ways my home had fallen short.

 I strove to take control and create order over every square inch of my home. I organized underwear and pyjama drawers. I put my children's clothes into neatly folded piles or hung them in specific categories. But once the babies began to move and reach their pudgy hands up, my home began to resemble a kitchen junk drawer.

 One day as I opened one of my children's doors from nap time, I broke down crying as I saw every bit of clothing thrown around the room and each basket of categorized toys dumped into one pile. I tried to help him clean it, but when he couldn't make sense of my system or fold a t-shirt properly, I cast him away and put it all back to order on my own as tears soaked my neckline.

 "You must have been exhausted," someone said to me after I told them the story.

 "I was," I replied. "I work so hard to keep this home clean, and then it seems like someone is going behind me and undoing it all."

 She nodded. "Well, he is old enough now that maybe it could be a consequence that he has to clean up the mess when he does something like this."

 I shook my head and chuckled.

"No, never. He doesn't know how to fold clothes and he doesn't understand the system I've created for storing the toys."

She tilted her head to the side. "Why does that matter? What if he just shoved it all wherever it fit?"

I furrowed my face. My heart quickened. "What? Then it's not in order, it's not put away right, and the drawers will be a mess—"

"But why does that matter? It's his stuff and he's the one who has to deal with the lack of organization."

I shook my head fiercely. "No, no, no. I can't do that. What if someone saw?"

She shrugged. "So what?"

My bottom lip trembled. "If they saw, they'd believe I was a horrible mother."

"What do you mean?" she said.

Tears stung my eyes. "The only thing making me a good mother is this home. If it falls apart, I'm unfit."

That conversation began my healing. I realized my obsessive compulsions for order and my tidiness originated in the belief that my goodness as a person was represented by the order of my home. I equated my justification as a mom with the cleanliness of my living space. This is where I should tell you that you're a good mom regardless of all these things—you're a good mom because you're trying hard. But that's not the case. For the believer, you're a good mom because Jesus is your righteousness and the Holy Spirit is carving you more and more into the likeness of Christ.

I'm a checklist person, someone who always strives for the best grades to prove my worth. Give me a rule and I'll put up fence posts so I don't come near to surpassing it. Even as a believer, I tried writing a bulleted list of things I had to do to be a good Christian—and missing one of those tasks left me ridden with guilt.

Yet Jesus says, "Come to me, all who labor and are heavy laden, and I will give you rest. Take my yoke upon you, and learn from me, for I am gentle and lowly in heart, and you will find rest for your souls. For my yoke is easy, and my burden is light" (Matt.

11:28–30 ESV). How can Jesus say such a thing when the law towers above us and our dirty floors cry out below us? Because he has completed the work for our justification. In his thirty-something years on earth, Jesus fulfilled the law on our behalf. He lived the perfect life we could not so that he would be the perfect sacrifice for our sins (not needing to pay for his own). Then he gave us his righteousness as he took on our depravity while nailed to the cross.

Yet Jesus not only died for our justification but for our sanctification as well. He promised that when he left, he'd send along a better gift than his earthly presence: The Holy Spirit dwelling within each believer, sanctifying them into Christlikeness. Paul wrote to the Galatians that we are not perfected by our flesh but by the Holy Spirit, just as we are not saved by works of the law but by faith (Gal. 3:1–9). Pastor and author John Fonville once said in a sermon, "Do you know how many people believe that sanctification is their work? 'God gets you in by grace, but you keep and complete yourself by your work or your cooperation with grace.' That's not the gospel, and that's not how it works. Sanctification is the work of God's free grace."[11]

This doesn't mean we do nothing. Like the servants who were entrusted with their master's talents, we are called to be faithful with what we are given (Matt. 25:14–30). We are told to be righteous as our Heavenly Father is righteous (1 Pet. 1:15–17). Yet we will never justify ourselves before God or make ourselves holy. We are declared righteous by the work of Christ, and we are day by day, by ordinary means of the Word, fellow believers, suffering, and the sacraments, made righteous like Christ by the Holy Spirit.

There's so much unseen work in the life of a mother, and much of the work we pour into forming our children will take years

---

[11] Fonville, John. "The Gospel Mystery of Sanctification, Part 2." *Paramount Church* (sermon), September 8, 2019. https://www.paramountchurch.com/sermons/sermon/2019-09-08/the-gospel-mystery-of-sanctification-part-2.

before we see any fruit. Few to none see the days of discipline, the hours of reading, the quiet teaching moments in the front yard, or the millions of seconds we spend on our knees pushing trains on wooden tracks. How many people see us scrubbing the walls with poop painted on them, walking through the mud flats to retrieve a favorite stick, or the endless time spent at the table taping beloved books back together. Yet our homes can be a place where we feel as if our goodness, rightness, and worthiness can be displayed for all to see. They see the shine and sheen, the fresh paint and trendy decor, the clean bedspreads and empty laundry baskets. We can trust people to affirm our efforts as they take a tour throughout the place we've cultivated.

Yet this is also exhausting work, even without children. Once we unleash little ones upon our nurtured homes, the sweat we dripped over our interior design is quickly undone or mutilated. Vases break, toys puncture and dent walls, and windows gain a veil of fingerprints. It's not lasting.

As I drive through the more historic parts of our community, I often grieve when I see what was once a lovely home with multiple full levels and elegant carvings gracing the exterior hidden behind years of unmowed grass with broken windows and chipped paint. Someone once poured their heart and soul into this home with pride and joy, and now it's a lawsuit waiting to happen that nobody wants to pay to tear down. When we turn our van up our driveway, I can't help but wonder if or when the same will become of my beloved home and what purpose all my efforts even matter. Yet God calls us to a better purpose for our homes.

Though God doesn't need our good works, Martin Luther the Reformer declared, our neighbor does. God calls us to use our homes to bring glory to him by serving our neighbors in such a way that we showcase the gospel to them—not our skills as home decorators. By opening our doors (no matter what they look like) with grace, compassion, and selfless love, we mirror our Savior who opened heaven for all those who put their faith in him. We reflect Jesus as he sat down with the poor, the needy, the ailing, and the unwanted.

As we slowly work to transform our hearts from viewing our homes as a place to prove ourselves, the anxiety gradually releases its python grip on us. Suddenly it's not the speck of dust that might make someone judge our goodness that bothers us, but how much attentiveness we're giving to the image bearer sitting before us. When we find our justification and sanctification as moms in Christ rather than our works (like the tidiness of our houses), sitting down to rest during housework isn't shameful. It's an act of trust as we release what's left to God to close our eyes and sleep.

13
Learning Courage

No coward soul is mine,
No trembler in the world's storm-troubled sphere:
I see Heaven's glories shine,
And faith shines equal, arming me from fear.
O God within my breast,
Almighty, ever-present Deity!
Life—that in me has rest,
As I—undying Life—have power in Thee!

— Emily Brontë, Last Lines

As our van turned into the dirt parking lot of our church, I wanted to whirl it back around to the highway. The steeple towered above us as we settled into a parking space between two other vehicles. All the while, my stomach wrenched inside me, and threatened to vomit my breakfast onto the carpeted floor. Tremors shook me.

I gripped the armrests and closed my eyes.

"I can't do this," I cried. I had no strength left within me to enter another social situation where anxiety wrapped its hands around my throat.

My husband reached over and held my hand. "We can go home. It's up to you."

My heart pounded like the wings of a hummingbird. I looked up at the people trickling in through the open glass doors of our church. More tears tumbled from my cheeks, leaving little splatters on my jeans.

I clamped my hand over the door handle and pushed it open. Without a word, we unbuckled the children and strode across the gravel toward the greeter. With every step, I wanted to turn and bolt, to go anywhere but a building crowded with people.

All three of my kids have a bit of shyness to them, just like I've always had. Some weeks, to my great surprise, I drop them off at the church nursery and they run inside without a peep. Other times, they cling to our clothes and scream that they don't want to go.

As their mom, I felt that anxiety too.

As we walked the carpeted floors, I pressed one of the twins to my side and gripped my oldest's hand so people wouldn't see it shaking. I swallowed hard against both my gag reflex and the lump swelling in my throat, trying to keep my bottom lip from quivering. Every moment of eye contact, a smile, or a wave ignited a desire to run out the glass doors as I towed my children in the opposite direction to the nursery.

I led my oldest to the sign-in desk, and he shook his head and cowered behind my legs.

"Nooo," he said, shoving his face between my knees.

"You don't want to go?" I replied. My voice trembled.

He shook his head again, hitting it into my buckling legs.

Daniel stepped up next to me with a cup of coffee sloshing in his hands. "You ready?" he asked. He bent down towards our son. "Let's get you ready to go into the nursery to play!" he said.

But our oldest turned away from him and clung to my legs even tighter.

"Let's just bring him into the service with us," I said, turning towards the door.

Daniel frowned. "But he struggles to get through the service.

He'll have more fun there."

I took in a shaky breath. "Just forget it," I hissed under my breath. Without another word, I speed-walked out the door and towards the large open doors of the sanctuary.

Daniel was irritated, but I was relieved. Having all my children with me in the service meant I could flee back to our van and drive home with them at any moment I chose without delay.

Social anxiety poked its head in and out of my life, like a squirrel gathering nuts for the winter. At times I could stand alone on a stage to recite lines and read my poetry. Other times, I could barely attend school without panic attacks dissolving me into a quivering puddle of water.

During those months around the incident at church, my anxiety ran and roamed about in my life rather than staying quiet in its burrow. Attending church suffocated me. Every siren in my body screamed at the highest volume. My knees threatened to let go under me. My stomach boiled. I desired to speak brave words to my children to give them courage; I wanted to untie a ribbon of faith from my heart and braid it around theirs, but I didn't have any of my own to give. All these years I still didn't have my step-by-step action plan to conquer this fear.

Meanwhile, the faint memories and pictures of life before this extreme bout of anxiety haunted me as I remembered how much easier it used to be to leave the house prior to this season of more intense anxiety, and I wondered when or if that normalcy would ever return.

God must have rows of my bottled tears by now—tears that I shed over my anxiety when I begged him to take it all away. Yet the anxiety remained. I don't understand why, and in those moments of looking at my life and pondering why God's hand has not lifted the anxiety from me, doubt snaked around my heart. *Where is God's love? Why has he abandoned me?* Hyperventilating in the van, gagging in the bathroom, pacing in the basement, sobbing in my bedroom—each time I begged God for relief, and he said no. Each time I fought and pressed on, trying to keep myself from drowning in the whirlpool of anxiety. That day in the van, I didn't have any fight left in me. As the anxiety swirled in my body and mind, I felt as though I was caught in the bathtub drain, and I didn't have the breath or strength to keep swimming against its currents.

Months of anxiety led up to that day in the van. I had fought back, plowed through, and wrangled every tool therapy had given me. Yet still it raged; still, it threatened to drown me. With each outing, I felt like its grip grew ever stronger.

I wanted courage. As a little girl, I read and wrote stories about characters more courageous than I could ever dream, and consumed stories of missionaries and martyrs who never balked at the thought of dying for Jesus. I hoped that by reading these stories, I could learn the same kind of courage.

I learned that courage isn't pressing forward without any fear (that's just normal life). Courage is storming the castle while fear bangs its fists on the doors of our hearts, crying for us to retreat. But if the fear remains, where do we find courage? How do we keep moving our feet forward and keep our swords raised? Reflecting on courage in children's fairy tales, Vigen Guroian writes,

> Courage also needs the ground of ultimate trust on which to stand and act—something or someone who embodies goodness and truth wholly and unqualifiedly. Then it may deepen into a courage to be wholly for others and to risk the self in their behalf. Authentic courage, therefore, makes use of faith and love—or, rather, it fulfills itself in faith and love through selfless and unselfish acts of being for others.[12]

Courage grows from two branches of love—the first branch is faith that someone greater loves us despite what happens and will not abandon us in our time of need. George MacDonald said that the highest condition of the human will is that when not seeing God or

---

[12] Vigen Guroian, *Tending the Heart of Virtue*, Second (New York, NY: Oxford University Press, 2023), 146.

seeming to grasp him at all, we still hold fast to him.[13] We find the will, the courage, to press forward in spite of fear because we believe we have taken hold of God's hand that already held us, even when every feeling declares he's not there. Courage comes when we take God at his Word, trusting that he truly walks with us through the valley of the shadow of death.

The second branch of courage grows out as an offspring from faith in God's love: a love for another. We see this kind of courage in Sam Gamgee as he walked through the gates of Mordor alone, fighting orcs along the way, to save his beloved friend Frodo. He could complete the mission by himself or try to run home, but he chose to go to the most forsaken and darkest stronghold because he knew his friend lived imprisoned within those walls.

We see it in *Jane Eyre*, when Jane, despite her deep love for Mr. Rochester, refuses to marry him when she discovers he is already married. In great courage, she flees from his estate because her love for God and his law is greater than her love for Rochester. When we love someone else greater than our fears, especially when that love is strengthened by resting in the relentless love of God, we can brace our feet rather than flee in the face of fear.

For years, I tried to bootstrap my courage, to dig up something from within to make me fearless. I tried to use shame, selfishness, and self-preservation, but they all created a distorted and flimsy version of courage that never lasted. I needed to grab hold of the divine love of Christ as my Good Shepherd, which I found during another morning at church.

As the church announcements began, I hushed my three boys and gathered them into our row of seats. Within a few minutes, the band was called forward and my husband stepped on stage with his banjo, leaving me on single-parent duty with an almost five-year-old and two two-year-olds.

---

[13] George MacDonald, "A Dish of Orts, by George MacDonald," ed. Jonathan Ingram, Sandra Brown, and David Widger, The Project Gutenberg, September 29, 2003, https://www.gutenberg.org/files/9393/9393-h/9393-h.htm.

Today, the fear of vomiting that tangled with my social anxiety couldn't stand against my fear of judgment about my parenting abilities from all those watching my children run across the seats, stab the seats with pens, throw paper like confetti, and roll my metal water bottle under the seats. I sang the songs as the lyrics rolled across the screens at the front, but my head bobbed in every direction with each line sung as I wrestled a pen away from one child using it like a straw and dove for another running toward the emergency exit.

The relieving words from the pastor called out from the stage. "Alright, why don't you greet one another while the children head downstairs for Sunday School."

I sighed and began herding my little ones together in the side aisle, but an arm came over my shoulder and pulled me into a woman's side.

"Hi there, love," she said. Her dark, graying hair wisped around her face and tickled mine as she looked down at me. "I just wanted to say you're doing a great job."

The world seemed to pause. I blinked and stared at her.

"Listen, I sit behind you and I see your head swirling around like a spinning top in every direction, and I can't help but remember when that was me. I had three children too, and they were wild—ask anyone here today, or even your friend over there who went to school with them!" she laughed. "But listen: You're bringing them here, and that's what matters. And you know what? It's such a blessing to us to see them here to worship God. It's just such a light for my eyes to see little boys being boys. Keep it up, you're a great mom."

Words seemed to hang around me, but I struggled to grasp them. Instead, I hugged her while two of my boys rattled the emergency door behind me. "Thank you," I breathed. "You have no idea what that means to me."

My husband appeared behind me, and I realized the twins were nowhere in sight. I crunched my face.

A Mother Held

"Did you take the twins to the nursery?" I asked.

He nodded. "Yeah, but there was no one in there. The pastor's wife said she would stay there with them."

"Oh." Guilt pricked my heart; I couldn't leave her down there alone with who knows how many kids, including my busy twins. I glanced down at my oldest son, who had hidden behind my legs like curtains. "Do you want to go to the nursery with me?"

He fiercely nodded his head and took my hand. We jogged down the narrow stairs and stepped through the half-door of the nursery, where the kind pastor's wife and her eighteen-month-old daughter sat with my two boys. "I can help," I said, giving my son a tap on the back to go play.

Throughout that hour, we shared about motherhood, pursuing creativity as a mom of little ones, raising wild boys, and how they all grow inexplicably slow and fast at the same time. That Sunday, a smile pulled at my face that I couldn't quite make sense of; I still can't express the way that Sunday settled inside me. It left me a warmth that didn't come from the muggy weather preparing the sky for a storm—I felt courageously whole, a feeling I couldn't remember feeling last.

Rather than trying to force myself to attend church for appearances or to get my needed socialization in for the week, I climbed into the van with a desire to behold and serve my Savior that morning. Then I branched out from that love and looked to my family—they not only needed to behold and serve their Savior too but see me step forward in faith as well. If I want my children to believe in the necessity of church and see their place in the body of Christ, I need to first walk by example for them.

This didn't extinguish my fears; my stomach still roils like a boiling pot of soup at times. But I found courage, and I had enough to share. Some days, when I walk stiffly to the nursery with my little ones in tow, I feel their anxiety. Each Sunday, I'm learning to pray this for myself and them:

Even though we feel as if we're walking through the valley of the shadow of death, teach us to bring our every fear to you, and believe that you are with us. Help us to find comfort in your rod and your staff, for we know they protect us as we go forward. You are our Shepherd. Please restore our souls.

This is the heart of courage. Not absence of fear, not grinning and bearing, not looking deep within, not just believing in ourselves. It's looking and reaching outside of ourselves—first towards Heaven, then towards our fellow man.

14
No Gold Stars for Burnout

> *There is a self-love which is corrupt, and the root of the greatest sins, and it must be put off and mortified; but there is a self-love which is the rule of the greatest duty: we must have a due concern for the welfare of our own souls and bodies. And we must love our neighbour as truly and sincerely as we love ourselves.*
>
> — Matthew Henry[14]

I was fifteen years old, working as a cabin leader at a Christian summer camp. A last-minute change of plans for our day had led the entire camp to the shoreline for lunch and swimming for over two hours. Part way through the time, I was scheduled for my one, sixty-minute break of the day. I asked if I could return to the lodge when the time came for my break.

The director said no.

As the reverberations of the shock rippled through me, I shook my head and swallowed. I apologized and asked if I could take my break at a more convenient time.

The director rolled her eyes and scoffed. "No. I don't think you need a break from sitting on the beach."

---

[14] Mathew Henry, Zondervan NIV Matthew Henry Commentary In One Volume, ed. Leslie F. Church and Gerald W. Peterman (Grand Rapids, MI: Zondervan Publishing House, 1992), 119.

My face burned. I looked away from her rolling eyes. It felt as if my already small body had shrunk several sizes before her. I don't remember even nodding or saying another word; I just slunk away.

The next day, we gathered in the staff lounge for a meeting. The director pointed at one of my fellow cabin leaders. "There's someone you should emulate!"

I looked over at the girl sitting in the corner of the fraying armchair. She smiled and looked down at her hands, bashful. I saw dark circles under her eyes.

The camp director held her hand up toward the girl. She told us how this counselor had been going straight for two days and didn't take a single break. Her eyes glared at each of us as she scoffed about how we couldn't clamber in here fast enough when the clock ticked to our break time. Her tirade continued as she straightened to take the pose of a preacher behind a pulpit. We needed to realize this summer wasn't about us because we weren't working an ordinary job; our work was meant to bring children to Jesus. Because of that, we needed to stop idolizing our breaks.

I looked away. The incident with the shoreline was the second or third time that summer I had asked about getting a break I had missed. I scowled at myself. I was a failure, a selfish failure. I should have gritted my teeth and pressed on. Where's my selflessness? Where's my cross-carrying? I fought back tears for the rest of the meeting. I never wanted to be called out like that again. I wanted people to see my holiness, not my self-absorption.

Almost ten years later with camp days behind me, I looked at the red numbers on the digital clock on top of our bureau again. It couldn't be right, could it? But what else should I have expected?

A Mother Held

I had forty-five minutes to sleep—and then I'd have to do the whole breastfeeding process over again.

I was twenty-four years old, a mom to a three-year-old son and newborn twin boys. Every two hours, our twins needed to be woken up to breastfeed. They took anywhere from thirty to sixty minutes to eat, and then I had to pump and supplement for the smaller one. After that, I had to clean and sterilize all the breast pump equipment so it would be ready for the next feeding.

As I sat on the edge of the bed, a whine that escalated into a wail echoed down the hallway.

I looked at my husband sitting at the foot of the bed next to me. "I can't do it," I said.

Hysteria rose in my chest and coated my words. "I can't do it. My life is lived out in forty-five-minute increments. I can't live like this." My words choked out into sobs.

Every time I laid my head down, stepped in the shower, or microwaved a meal, I heard babies screaming—sometimes real, sometimes imagined. If I laid my head down for a nap, I jolted awake five minutes later, my heart thumping in my chest, because I thought I had forgotten to feed my babies.

"I'll settle them," he said, "you lay down."

I did, I didn't even dare resist. The babies settled quickly, but I lay awake long after my husband curled up behind me, my brain unable to stop processing, like a computer stuck with a twirling loading bar. My brain circled and circled in shame—regret that I had not been the selfless mom to go down the hallway and care for her babies. I was the one with the milk after all. I had all they needed. Why had I even woken my husband up? I felt just like I did at camp; running from building to building, child to child, task to task, while my eyes burned and my limbs shook from low sugar. All to be more holy.

When slumber finally closed my eyes, we woke up forty-five minutes later and did it all over again.

As I clutched two babies to my chest again that night, I thought about what my obstetrician said before we left the hospital: She wanted me to get at least five hours of straight sleep once a day. I laughed hysterically at the thought while my husband snored next to me.

Perhaps you could supplement with formula, she had said. *That way someone else can feed the babies while you sleep.*

Formula? That was poison. And me, *sleep?* I was the mother. How could I be so selfish? How could I feed my babies formula while liquid gold filled my breasts for them?

I jumped as one of the twins squeezed my breast. I flinched and squinted down at a bright red spot. The baby dozed off into a milk-drunk slumber while an infection began to rage.

I stood in my bedroom with my cell phone pressed up against my cheek. Babies and a toddler screamed in another room while my breast bellowed with pain. Another clog had turned into another infection. Over the past four months, I had consistently gotten mastitis every two weeks—and each time it took a week to fully recover. "How likely is it that these infections will keep happening?" I asked the doctor.

My doctor sighed. "It will likely keep happening until you stop breastfeeding."

I squeezed my eyes shut. "Do you think..." I winced as I readjusted my breast, feeling the prickles of milk filling it up. "Do you think I should switch to formula?"

"I do." She explained the reality I already knew but didn't want to admit: that I could not care for my family while facing this kind of illness every other week. She seized the truths I had batted away for days and laid them out plainly before me. So, with my throbbing chest bound up in sports bras, I cradled only one of my infants to feed him formula in a bottle. Across from me, I watched with hot rage while my mother-in-law cuddled the other twin as he guzzled down the off-white liquid. Not rage at her; rage at my weakness.

That is supposed to be me—only I should be feeding him with my breastmilk! I swallowed against the jagged rock swelling in my throat. *You weakling—you pathetic excuse for a mother! How could you give up so easily? How many other moms would have sacrificed and pushed through? What a failure. Your body couldn't push them out at birth, and now your breasts can't feed them.* I squeezed my eyes shut. I saw myself no better than my fifteen-year-old self on that muggy summer day at camp.

I stared down into the endless brown eyes of my smallest baby as he sucked down the strange-smelling milk and I fought my trembling lip.

I picked the bottle out of the hot mug of water, my eyelids sagging. I could barely hold the chubby baby on my hip. Then a family friend scooped both the child and formula from my grasp.

"You go rest," she said. "Your mother-in-law and I will feed them."

I gingerly reached out my hand. "But... they're my babies."

She laughed. "Yes, they are still your babies. And to be their mother, you need to sleep."

I opened my mouth, then closed it. She smiled and bounced the little twin to the living room where my mother-in-law sat, already propped up in a rocking chair with the other twin. I sighed and dragged my feet to the bedroom. I laid down in the bed, not even bothering to draw the curtains or move the decorative pillows. I curled up on my side and stared at the wall, my eyes burning like they were covered in sand.

I closed my eyes and woke up hours later.

I ran from the bedroom to the living room. The family friend and my mother-in-law sat on the floor with the twins while they cooed and wiggled on a blanket.

"I'm so sorry," I gasped, running a hand over my hair to smooth it. "I didn't realize—"

They both laughed and waved their hands. "It's okay," the family friend said. "That's why we said you could rest." She raised an eyebrow at me. "How do *you* feel?"

I stood still for a moment. I blinked. My eyes felt normal. My head felt clearer. My chest didn't feel as compressed. I didn't feel like crying.

"I feel…" I let my shoulders fall and smiled. "Better."

I crept out of the nursery room after laying down the twins and curled up in a chair across from my husband's aunt who had come over to help me with the twins.

"I saw a photo on Instagram the other day," I said, "of a mom with triplets. She had them each propped up with pillows and fed them all at the same time—a bottle in each hand and one balanced with her foot!" I laughed and swallowed the words I didn't say. *What a failure I am—I need help to take care of only two infants and a toddler.*

Her face scrunched as she tsked. "Oh my," she replied, "that sounds like such a sad situation. That's a mom without a good support system."

Her words struck me. I had shared that photo with several other people, all of whom laughed in amazement like me. But she didn't see it the same: she saw a mom who needed help.

I smiled a little. *A mom like me.*

A Mother Held

With a baby on my hip, I lifted the formula bottle from the sink and dripped some of it on my wrist to check the temperature. Though it didn't need to be heated, one of the twins wanted his formula as hot as his little mouth could handle.

My in-laws hired two homeschooled girls to help me around the house and care for my three little ones during the week while my husband worked. I passed her one of the bottles, shaking off some of the boiled water. We both walked out to the living room, each snuggling and cooing with a baby in our arms. We laughed as the twins strained and pulled as much as they could on the bottles, their mouths wide like baby birds.

As I settled into the wingback chair and glanced over at the young girl feeding one of the twins beside me, a sting of shame pricked me for a moment—the same sickening feeling in the pit of my stomach like that day as a cabin leader. Yet when I looked down at my sweet baby and listened to his grunts as he gulped down the store-bought formula, I knew I had not only made the right choice but the most selfless choice too. While my heart had pridefully fought for self-sufficiency and to prove my holiness as a mom to the world with burn-out, I chose to resist that temptation and submit to the bottle—ultimately, to God.

I believed rest sat on the same line as the sin of sloth, while exhaustion, burn-out, bleary eyes, and pained muscles were all equated with holiness. Yet it's our perfect Creator who created the Sabbath day and declared it holy. After creating everything that scuttles and flies, swims and herds, and grows tall with fruit, God rested. Most of us know this story and know its place in the table of the law.

We see God enforcing this law and the breaking of it often through the Israelites' story. While the Israelites traveled through the wilderness on their way to the Promised Land, they complained about their lack of food. To fill their stomachs, God sent manna, a bread-like substance that fell from heaven. Each morning, the manna appeared on the ground and the Israelites had to gather enough for the day because any leftovers would rot. But on the sixth day, things went a bit differently:

> On the sixth day they gathered twice as much bread, two omers each. And when all the leaders of the congregation came and told Moses, he said to them, 'This is what the Lord has commanded: "Tomorrow is a day of solemn rest, a holy Sabbath to the Lord; bake what you will bake and boil what you will boil, and all that is left over lay aside to be kept till the morning"' (Exod. 16:22–23 ESV).

On the sixth day, God allowed enough manna to be persevered for the following day so they could rest on the Sabbath. As per usual, the Israelites tried to go their way: some wandered out to gather on the Sabbath and found nothing.

God didn't put the Sabbath in place to control us. Rather, it's because we're not limitless creatures with the ability to run and work without taking breaks. God purposely made us finite, requiring rest, food, shelter, and help from the community. For that reason, God established the Sabbath by resting on the seventh day of creation. He didn't need the rest but instead set up a pattern for us to follow (Gen. 2:1–3). Sometimes obedience looks like resting when we want to do good work. Rest requires trust and faith that God can work while we rest.

God provides a beautiful picture of the gospel through the Sabbath day. Just as I need physical rest because of my finitude, I also require spiritual rest to save me from my sin.

I tried to save myself by keeping the law but failed. Yet God, rich in mercy, sent Jesus to pay the full penalty for my sins while I received his righteousness. I can rest secure in his finished work rather than striving in the impossible toil of fulfilling the law on my own.

A Mother Held

I crossed my legs that day and leaned back in the chair as my baby drank drowsily. I allowed my shoulders to drop and my head to rest. With my toddler in his room for quiet time, I thought about how I might spend my own quiet time once the twins went to sleep.

I was badly in need of a haircut—longer hair meant more fuzz when it rained and more opportunity for my fourteen-month-olds to yank strands out with their tiny fists. I found a hair salon that worked nights and booked myself an appointment after the kids' bedtime.

As we drove the darkened highway, I kept up a volleyball game in my mind with shame. Should I spend the extra money to go into town to get a haircut? I already asked our in-laws to help so often—was it wrong that I asked for an evening to get my hair cut too? Perhaps I should have waited longer. Not only that, I had asked my husband to drive me out, despite being tired from a full day of work. Was it all just selfish?

Thirty minutes later, my husband dropped me off at the salon. The place smelled of hairspray and perfume. My heels clunked along the hardwood floors to the reception desk where a girl possibly younger than me escorted me to her chair. I sat down in the leather chair in front of the large mirror; it towered above me with an intricate gold frame from the floor and vainly reached for the ceiling.

I met my green eyes in the reflection. My eyes were darkened with exhaustion and my sprigs of gray hair glittered in the yellow lights. My complexion was pale. I saw someone in need of more than a haircut. Like Bilbo, "I feel all thin, sort of stretched, if you know what I mean; like butter that has been scraped over too much bread. That can't be right. I need a change, or something."[15]

---

[15] J. R. R. Tolkien, *The Fellowship of the Rings*, of *The Lord of the Rings* (London, England: Harper Collins Publishers, 2007), 42.

I struggled to rest. Any time I took to rest or recover, I always felt selfish and shameful. Because of this, I often pushed through, gritted my teeth against aching muscles, pried my drooping eyes open, and put my head down to plow forward. But the week prior, my body forced me to stop. I balled my fists and clenched my jaw but my body gave way to crippling anxiety.

My body said no, and I had to stop.

I worked at Christian summer camps three summers in a row in high school where I learned a lot about rest and godliness—but not in a good way. We worked from 7:00 a.m. to 9:00 p.m. every day with one sixty-minute break; and if the kids were up at night, we worked then too. One night, I stayed up until three in the morning with a camper and my bosses expected me to work the usual day the next morning. They taught me that desperately grappling for and fighting for my single break was selfish for someone who was supposed to be serving God and caring for children. If I missed my break, I should simply accept it. Don't ask for a time to reschedule it—press on and sacrifice. That's the godly way—that's the way to holiness.

At fifteen years old, I hadn't considered how Jesus withdrew from the crowds to rest and I forgot about him sleeping in the boat during the storm. Those moments didn't make our perfect, sinless Savior any less holy—it's impossible. I likewise didn't know the story of Elijah running from his God-given mission field out of fear and exhaustion and how God fed him and gave him sleep. God never condemned his human needs or removed his holy calling, but enabled him to continue forward. God stooped to meet Elijah in his finitude. At fifteen, I didn't understand that my limitations were God-given and therefore good.

Through a beloved friend and mentor, God took me by the shoulders, looked me square in the eyes, and taught me about the good limitations he gave me and the beauty of the church carrying one another when we can't take another step further.

A Mother Held

This lesson had been further confirmed again as I read through Professor Kelly Kapic's book, *You're Only Human*. He writes, "Many of us fail to realize that our limitations are a gift from God, and therefore good. This produces in us the burden of trying to be something we are not and cannot be."[16] He goes on, "Denying our finitude cripples us in ways we don't realize. It also distorts our view of God and what Christian spirituality should look like."[17]

God is teaching me that without rest, I can't be who he's called me to be and fulfill his law properly. I'm learning to respect the limits God wisely gave me—not fight against them like they're imperfections and mistakes. I also want to model to my children a healthy lifestyle and how trusting God sometimes means leaving the dishes and taking a nap—or booking a hair appointment and calling a babysitter. Bilbo was right—we're not meant to feel like butter stretched too thin. The nature of motherhood and all of life will at times leave us feeling that way, but it should never be our constant or normal habit of life.

Being eternal, our good God offers us eternal life. By putting our faith in his Son's work on the cross, we can spend eternity in unbroken harmony with this awesome God. No more tears, no more weariness, no more aching muscles. When we feel weak and frustrated by how limited we are, we can turn to him and find rest, knowing he has taken care of all we need for salvation in the gospel. Don't you see? This rest is holy—God not only commands it but reflects a picture to us of the good news he offers us. We don't need to work without ceasing to prove our worth to our Father because Christ has already accomplished all we need for salvation. He never scoffs at our need to rest but meets us in our needs. We can now serve God out of a place of rest and gratitude. And until our eternal rest, we can set boundaries and practices to help us steward our time and energy to God's glory.

---

[16] 1. Kelly Kapic, *You're Only Human: How Your Limits Reflect God's Design and Why That's Good News* (Grand Rapids, MI: Brazos Press, 2022), 3.
[17] Kapic, 6.

15

He Will Hold Me Fast

I know thy grace doth still for wanderers look;
I was a lost sheep once; dear Lord, behold,
And in compassion take me with thy hook.
In one lost sheep new found, thou dost rejoice;
Then know thy sheep, which know his Shepherd's
voice.

— Henry Constable

When my oldest was a baby, I paced the floors for hours while trying to soothe him. In darkened rooms before the sun rose, in the living room where dust danced like fairies in the light that stretched between the curtains, and in the church basement as the congregation sang and listened above me. He had reflux and didn't sleep well, and I was a first-time mom with barely a clue of what I was doing.

As my arms ached and exhaustion made my eyes burn like sand, my shaky voice put itself into a hymn.

When I fear my faith will fail
Christ will hold me fast
When the tempter would prevail
He will hold me fast

A Mother Held

As I paced over creaky, uneven floorboards, my soul clung to the truth I needed most: That Christ will hold me fast through it all. I feared for my mind which seemed to become more and more clouded with darkness each day—intrusive thoughts I didn't understand, fears of inadequacy, and a cloak of sadness that weighed on me—and my physical health that was beginning to feel all the ramifications of lack of sleep, lack of food, and fluctuating hormones.

In the midst of it all, my faith appeared as a fraying thread. I could barely catch five minutes to read my Bible and most Sunday mornings I spent wandering the church basement or holed up in another room breastfeeding.

But as I paced, I reached out to get my hands around the one thing I knew I could: a beloved hymn I could sing to my crying babe. Some days I cried with him as I sang the words. Some days my foggy brain couldn't remember all the lines, so I hummed the melody. And Christ carried me through, like the lost sheep, and didn't let me go.

> *I could never keep my hold*
> *Through life's fearful path*
> *For my love is often cold*
> *He must hold me fast*

The loss of our two babies to miscarriage rattled my faith in ways I wasn't expecting. How could God take two unborn babies from my womb? How could he allow my joy to be crushed nearly in the same breath? And not just once, but twice? To add salt to the wound, weeks after the babies had left me, I still found myself curled up on the couch with nausea.

Where is God? I demanded of my friends and husband. *Where is this good God who claims to love me? How could he stand by and allow this?* I clenched my fists and shook them at God.

Every promise I read in Scripture ignited embers of anger in the pit of my chest. How could both my heartache and his love be true?

Yet a dear friend sent me the lines of the hymn I had held so near:

> Those He saves are His delight
> Christ will hold me fast
> Precious in His holy sight
> He will hold me fast
> He'll not let my soul be lost
> His promises shall last
> Bought by Him at such a cost
> He will hold me fast

I wept as I read the words. Like everyone else, she didn't know the answers, but she did know what remained true: Christ would hold me fast because he loved me. As I wrestled through doubt and anger, I realized that while I was demanding an answer from God to prove his love for me, I had forgotten his greatest act of love on the cross. He redeemed me with his own life, was crushed for my iniquities, bore the unbearable wrath of God that I deserved—how could he not love me? This world is broken, but he promises to hold me fast through it all until he redeems each of his children and renews his marred creation.

I stood in the shower, water washing away my tears and its rushing noise covering my sobs, wrenching out word after word of this hymn. *Will he? Will he truly hold me fast? Is he holding me right now, even though I feel so empty and crushed?* I wondered this with every refrain. I sought to stifle my weeping as I got dressed and brushed my teeth. *Oh God, you must. After all you've done, how could you not?*

One day, as one of my twins cried from a fever and stuffy nose (and the other cried for him), I gathered them up in the rocking chair with me to sing that same song. They still cried, and I wept again with them. My oldest played and listened from the couch. Christ carried each of us through.

Each moment I've held one of my babies over the past four years, Christ has cradled me. When they cried out in the night and I struggled to lift my head from the pillow, Christ followed me to their darkened room and listened to my cries.

As I comforted my children from stomach aches and monsters behind the curtains, Christ comforted me. While I held them fast, he held each of us.

When we close our eyes for the final time on this earth, he will draw each of his children to eternal life, where our faith will be made sight as we behold the One who carried us through every heartache, every trouble, every wandering, every tossing of the sea. While we wait, he'll not let us be lost; he'll pursue us, and he'll surely hold us fast to that beautiful day. You are his delight and precious in his sight—Christ will hold you, even when your failing hands can hold onto nothing else.

> Raised with Him to endless life
> He will hold me fast
> Till our faith is turned to sight
> When he comes at last

When the twins were infants, I felt like I was in a tailspin at times; we woke every two hours to feed and pump, sterilized and filled bottles, changed endless diapers, and had a toddler struggling with the new changes. My anxiety created a riptide in my mind that tried to suck me under at every turn with intrusive thoughts and flashbacks to my traumatic delivery.

Even singing a hymn to them felt like grasping at the air.

I didn't have the courage to find those words this time—I could barely tell an intrusive thought from my own.

Through a string of unlikely circumstances, we were connected with a young girl who would come into my home to help me with my housework and children. Each day, she sang hymn after hymn to our babies—and in doing so, she sang them to me as well. She doesn't know, but her beautiful voice stringing out hymns from memory became a rock for me to cling to while the whirlpool pulled at my ankles. As we paced the floors with wailing babies, I took hold of every word she sang.

> *For my life He bled and died*
> *Christ will hold me fast*
> *Justice has been satisfied*
> *He will hold me fast*

When I couldn't sing, she sang for me. And by God's grace, I was held fast yet again.

16

Overlooking the Valley

> *Glory be to God for dappled things—*
> *For skies of couple-color as a brinded cow;*
> *For rose-moles all in stipple upon trout that swim;*
> *Fresh-firecoal chestnut-falls; finches' wings;*
> *Landscape plotted and pieced—fold, fallow, and plough;*
> *And all trades their gear and tackle and trim.*
> *All things counter, original, spare, strange;*
> *Whatever is fickle, freckled (who knows how?)*
> *With swift, slow; sweet, sour; adazzle, dim;*
> *He fathers-forth whose beauty is past change:*
> *Praise him.*
>
> — Gerald Manley Hopkins, *Pied Beauty*

I picked up *The Snow Child* by Eowyn Ivey one evening after the kids were in bed. I had sprinted through a handful of nonfiction books in the previous weeks, and I was looking forward to jumping into a novel again.

In the pages, I met Mabel: a middle-aged woman isolated in Alaska's frigid winter suffering under the chokehold of melancholy and childlessness. She and her husband had fled to Alaska to start a new life together, all on their own. Years of strained relationships with family and friends made her feel like an outsider, especially after many years of barrenness and a stillborn. She grew tired of the whispers and looks and wanted to get away. She thought perhaps she and her husband would grow closer through the isolation, but instead, they only grew further apart.

When her husband accepts the invitation to help another family, Mabel becomes flustered and irritated. She wanted to keep her distance from everybody so nobody could judge her or whisper about her inadequacies.

As I poured over her story, I found myself perturbed by Mabel. *Don't you realize that a big part of your sadness is from your lack of community?* I thought. *Community isn't easy, but we can't survive without them.*

As soon as the words strung themselves together in my mind, I caught myself.

I am Mabel.

Depression had hung over my head for weeks at that point. I felt as if I moved through a gray cloud and everything around me had become muted by its mist. Every thought got lost in the cloud, so I sat before my computer each day staring at the blinking cursor. My children wanted to play, but my energy dissipated into a scant dusting over my body and quickly blew away with each of their cries. I wept—at the food being spilled and children throwing tantrums and laundry piled on my bed. I feared this was what my life would look like forever. Yet as I read Mabel's story, I saw myself, and somehow her remedy even when I couldn't see it for myself.

In reflecting on Mabel's story, the fog cleared enough for me to see myself in her: I had pushed the community away because crippling anxiety made it feel far too dangerous to draw near to others or invite them into my home. In doing so, I made room for a great darkness to fall over my life. As Kelly Kapic writes in *Embodied Hope*, "The flame of the individual faith weakens when it is alone, but in the true community the fire of faith illumines the night."[18]

I needed others to help keep the flame of my faith burning.

Mabel almost recognizes her needs as she puts her hands into

---

[18] Kapic, *Embodied Hope*, 127.

the tilled earth to plant potatoes. She finds herself reflecting through tears on another hardship in her life: Her stillborn baby. Yet she again rallies herself together, blots her tears, and reminds herself, "She had survived then, hadn't she? Even when she had wanted to lie down in the night orchard and sink into a grave of her own, she had stumbled home in the dark, washed in the basin, and in the morning cooked breakfast for Jack."[19]

While Mabel didn't have her husband in those moments of her life, she had another family helping her limp along. Two of the Bensons, Esther and her youngest son, Garrett, stay on Mabel's farm to help her plant crop and care for her husband. When she lifted her tear-streaked, dirt-covered face, Garrett awkwardly offered his sleeve to wipe her tears as Esther took Jack for a walk to strengthen his muscles. Though she feels as if she's rallying herself, she has a scaffolding of others holding her in ways she refused to see.

In the last pages of the book, Mabel and her husband are thrown into another season of grief. As she sobs silently, she "knew that she would survive because she had once before."[20] She looks over to her husband, who she expects to walk away from her pain as he had every single time in the past, yet he sits down beside her and they cry together. She and her husband grieve and persevere *together*.

With tears in my own eyes, I saw my own desperate need: Not just to rally myself but to take hold of those around me. I wanted to pick myself up and press through, to pride myself on having done it all on my own, yet my weak limbs couldn't hold me up anymore. As I collapsed, I reached out to family and friends, who took hold of me in every way by comforting my heart and providing for my physical needs.

My husband came home from work to hold the screaming child. My in-laws built a play area outside to put my three toddlers in so I could more easily take them outside on my own. My friends helped me write a list of activities to do with my children to keep

---

[19] Eowyn Ivey, *The Snow Child* (New York, NY: Back Bay Books, 2012), 188.
[20] Ivey, 376.

them from screaming so much. Along with that, each of them comforted me and assured me I was not weak for reaching out.

As my local community drew around me, I was reminded of a greater reality: Christ brought me through my dark fog over the years, and he would do it again. He brought me through the grief of two miscarriages, severe postpartum depression, twelfth grade in which all my friends abandoned me, and more. While Mabel took courage in herself, I was reminded of the courage found in my Savior, who promises to never lose me (John 6:37–39; Heb. 13:5).

At the beginning of the book, Mabel contemplates suicide. She decides to walk across the thin ice and let nature sweep her away. Yet she safely makes it across the ice and back again. Mabel looks up at the horizon, and the author describes these thoughts: "It was beautiful, Mabel knew, but it was a beauty that ripped you open and scoured you clean so that you were left helpless and exposed if you lived at all."[21]

Like nature, I've discovered that beautifully crafted novels have this same power, and God used this piece of community to bring me through my grief. As the author writes the very words we couldn't articulate or were too afraid to even piece together in the secrecy of our minds, we cry and feel seen.

As they describe the wonder of nature and the wildness of the wilderness, we feel awed and reverent. As they spin a tale of forgiveness and reconciliation or good defeating evil, hope feels much more tangible. We are torn open, but even as we are, we are reminded that another soul on this planet knows the depth of this pain and yet can see hope within it.

As believers, even secular stories can stir our faith. We know that all truth, beauty, and goodness first come from God and are given to his creation as a gift of common grace. As we feel and see these realities within a novel, our eyes are drawn upward in worship of him, even amidst our suffering. He granted us the novel to

---

[21] Ivey, 9.

enlighten our darkness and crafted the beautiful words to cause our hearts to stop and feel something again. As Sarah Clarkson articulated with such loveliness in *This Beautiful Truth*:

> For beauty comes to us all in moments that unravel our cynical surety as our hearts seem to come apart at the touch of some odd slant of light on an evening walk. Or we hear the strained thread of some beloved old music that seems to break the spell of doubt. We read a novel, a story of someone who forgave or fought or hoped, and we feel something stir to life as precious, as fragile, as urgent as a newborn child within us. We are encountered by beauty, and suddenly the story of our grief seems to be the passing thing—that faint ghostly illusion that one day will melt the beams of great, inexorable love. My deep belief is that beauty has a story to tell, one that was meant by God to speak to us of his character and reality, meant to grip our failing hands with hope.[22]

Good novels take us on a journey—much unlike ours yet also much like it. They grip us with beauty, tell us of the truth, and give us hope that goodness is there too. This is the enlightening power of storytelling. Stories take the same fibers of suffering that entwine around our lives yet weave them away from us at a distance so we can see the greater tapestry they are a part of. We see all the individual colors and where one thread knots into the other, whereas with our own suffering, we become too familiar with our aches, longings, and sadness to know where it began.

As we crawl through the dank valley of black rocks, heavy mist, and icy winds, we can't see beyond it. We look up, but the clouds swarm together so we can't see the sunlight; we look forward, yet we can't see the end; we look backward, and all we can see is the path we've been on. Yet novels beckon us to climb up the steep mountainside of someone else's valley, and once we reach the top, they lift their arms out and show it to us from the peaks. Suddenly, it becomes easier to understand our trials a little bit better.

---

[22] Sarah Clarkson, *This Beautiful Truth: How God's Goodness Breaks Into Our Darkness* (Grand Rapids, MI: Baker Books, 2021), 22–23.

This is what *The Snow Child* did for me, and maybe another novel can do the same for you. It takes being willing to search for the beauty and the knowledge of God's greater story to discern the truth, beauty, and goodness he's given to another by his common grace. Stories are one of the many dappled and varied means that God reflects himself to us in this world.

We can often get stuck in ruts of believing that God can only work through one sort of thing, yet the psalmist wrote, "The heavens declare the glory of God, and the sky above proclaims his handiwork. Day to day pours out speech, and night to night reveals knowledge … Their voice goes out through all the earth, and their words to the end of the world" (Ps. 19:1–2, 4 ESV). In the words of the poet Gerald Hopkins, "All things counter, original, spare, strange" should cause us to praise his name. Stories are yet one of these ways that God casts light into our darkness and fog so we can see a bit better and take hold of the hope that is in front of us.

17
A Story Led Me Home Again

> *Sorry I'm late but I swam into a fishing net. I managed to escape, and I swam away and hid. I was lost, I was scared, but a story led me home again.*
>
> — *Tiddler: The Story-Telling Fish* by Julia Donaldson[23]

At ten years old, I ducked under the weathered wooden fence above and lifted my feet over the fraying silver rope below. The horses barely lifted their heads from the grass to take note of me, and then resumed their grazing. I followed the causeway my parents had made between the pond and the river, crossing to the small path between the briar patches.

All the while, I weaved stories in my mind and imagined them in front of me, talking to characters and leaping over puddles that I pretended were rushing rapids. When I returned inside hours later, I scribbled them down in notebooks or typed on the yellowed, family desktop computer.

This was my daily habit- whether it rained, snowed, or the sun scorched my neck. I even chose it over horseback riding sometimes. It's how I faced gossip from the mean girls, recovered

---

[23] Julia Donaldson. *Toddler: The Story-Telling Fish*. 2nd ed. Toronto, ON: Scholastic Canada, 2017.

from punches to the nose, and pulled the knives out of my back from my friend's betrayal.

At ten years old, I dreamed of being an author, and nothing else.

I pulled the sheets of my three-year-old's bed up to the headboard, but I yanked too hard and pulled them out from under the mattress. With tears brimming in my eyes, I shoved them back under the foot of the mattress. *Deep breath.* I didn't have time to cry—I still had to make my bed and finish boiling eggs for my husband and my son. Then I had to feed babies—again. After that, I'd prepare and clean up from lunch. I'd eat. I might have five minutes before the babies would need to nurse again.

That's if they slept the entire time. Usually, they slept for twenty minutes on a good day.

I swallowed against the jagged bump in my throat and walked out to the kitchen. I flicked the burner dial off and carried the tiny pot to the sink. Raising the steaming pot higher than needed, I purposely poured out the eggs into the sink and bent over the sink to cry.

"What's wrong, Lara?" my husband asked.

I watched the cracked eggs roll and wobble into the drain as steam escaped past them. "I want to be human," I murmured. "I don't want to be a milk machine anymore."

A few days later, I crossed the threshold of my office. A thin layer of dust coated my laptop, desk, and bookshelf. I lowered myself down into my chair in front of the antique desk.

After the egg incident, my husband and mother-in-law agreed to get me a sixty-minute break every day to do whatever I wanted. My husband often suggested I sleep, and my basket of laundry and dirt-sprinkled floors bellowed to me. Yet I sat down to

A Mother Held

write, even as my eyelids drooped. Whatever the cost, I had to write, because I didn't know what to think or how to function otherwise. My brain resembled a bag of unkempt yarn—loose ends flying about and knotted together without any seeming start or finish. Writing took loose ends and knit them together with one another to create something lovely, or at least wrapped them up into a ball for later. Without writing, I couldn't see the tapestry of my life, only the snarly skein.

I gently lifted the top. I squinted at the brightly lit screen. I opened Google Docs and poised my fingers above the keyboard as an infant screeched in the background.

For an entire hour, I stared at the blinking cursor. It demanded words. It threatened me.
Finally, it resolved to mock me.

I had no words in me.

My husband promised ideas would return, that I was just tired and out of practice. But every day, I sat before the white screen and fought back tears as the cursor laughed at me.

Five years prior, I walked from my home to my pastor's house to help his wife with her newborn twins and two toddlers. They had hired me to help around the house on the weekdays. Each week, my belly had grown a little more as my firstborn wiggled inside.

With my jacket pulled taut around my swollen stomach, I waddled alongside the road as cars slowed past me. Each day that I walked, images swirled in my head of a story. The paved road and litter-speckled ditch morphed into a thick forest of towering trees. I imagined elvish creatures and whimsical castles.

I smiled as I kicked stones in front of myself. It was fun to think about, but I knew I couldn't afford to think about it any more than on this walk. I had "real" work to do, which was caring for other people's kids while trying to make a side career in freelance writing Christian living articles. Storytelling was simply a piece of my past, a piece I no longer had time for.

I sat in front of the computer in my office again, an exhausted mom of a toddler and twin infants, the cursor blinking. Everything I had worked for, I had poured myself into these past six years, was gone. All of it. Drained from me. The articles had left me like the breast milk that had dried up in my chest weeks prior.

The cursor laughed. I steeled my gaze.

What if I wrote about that Elven girl? What if I wrote myself out of this like I did in every other painful time in my childhood? I wrote through the time my latest crush called me four-eyes, the friends who abandoned me amid my anxiety, the time my father called me retarded, and when I wondered if my parents' marriage was over. I processed each of those not by journaling but by crafting stories and poetry. If I could write through trials, perhaps I could write through this too.

I smiled at the cursor. And I typed.

"It's just for fun," I said. I walked alongside my husband as I pushed our four-year-old on his trike. He pushed the stroller with the twins alongside me.

"So you don't know what's going to happen?"

I laughed. "No. And I'm okay with that. I don't even care if I finish it. I just want to write and see where the characters take me."

Over two years, I wrote five fantasy novels this same way, and in each one, I can see the untangling of the threads I faced during those two years:

I wrote a story of a self-reliant Elven princess who must learn to rely not only on her beloved knights and friends but also strangers from other parts of her world to save her kingdom. Looking back, I see I'm Elven Princess Acacia needing to put off her pride and accept help from those around me, even those who I fear seeing my vulnerability.

The next story followed three characters—a human-turned-faery, a faery, and an elf—who all must learn the courage of truth, be able to question the world we were brought up in, and forgive even those who hurt us the most. I wrote that story as I came face-to-face with my past and wrestled with the call to forgiveness.

Another story followed two teens from very different parts of society as they were drawn into another world entirely. In order to bravely face the storms ahead, they had to help each other overcome their painful past that sought to define them.

Each of these stories reflected my life in another light where I learned to move forward in a way I may not have found otherwise.

I finished the story. And in the process, I learned to write about theology and ordinary faith again. I don't know if anything will come of that Elven manuscript or if it will ever be bound and sit on my bookcase. But I do know this: I lost my way, and writing a story brought me home again.

If you feel lost amidst the diapers, breast pumps or bottles, hourly feedings, or floors covered in dirt, give yourself space to breathe and pursue something you love again. As believers, we can get caught in the belief that everything we do must produce visible fruit such as income, a cleaner home, a nutritious meal, greater knowledge, or more muscle density. We forget that glorifying God comes not just from producing fruit but also from enjoying him (WSC Q. 1). As Brianna Lambert writes for *Christianity Today*,

> I've learned this lesson in my own hobby of decorating cakes. Sometimes when I grab my frosting tips and parchment bag to craft a dolphin cake for my daughter or a frosted fire truck for my sons, I wonder if I'm squandering my gifts. My mind floods with guilt. Should I be making money at this? Am I wasting valuable time? But a robust theology of leisure lifts those burdens and reminds me that no, I don't need to be chained to big results, and yes, I can simply wonder at the way icing stacks. God is at play in the world around me, and I get to worship him through something as small as a well-decorated cake.[24]

For me, this will almost always be stories. Stories have a way of turning me outward again when I become absorbed in my small world; they bend me back out to see my story in the grander picture of redemption, life, and hope. They not only reflect my struggles to me in a clearer way but also the people around me; they display people in another kind of light that suddenly helps me to make sense of their pain and perhaps why they caused me pain as well. Stories teach me sympathy, both with myself and others.

Go, and find the story—or cake, or paint brushes, or knitting needles—that will lead you back home again.

---

[24] Brianna Lambert, "Worship God: Start a Hobby," Christianity Today, January 16, 2020, https://www.christianitytoday.com/ct/2020/january-web-only/work-sabbath-worship-god-start-hobby.html.

18
Eyes on Today

The giant trees are bending
Their bare boughs weighed with snow.
And the storm is fast descending,
And yet I cannot go.
Clouds beyond clouds above me,
Wastes beyond wastes below;
But nothing drear can move me;
I will not, cannot go.

— Emily Brontë, Spellbound

I prayed over each pregnancy that I'd never hear that word—then five years later I heard it over the phone concerning one of the twins.

"Based on my evaluation, he qualifies for our autism program."

I felt like leaning over the sink to heave for air. Did I expect any other response? I had already endured two other over-the-phone questionnaires to put us on the waiting list for an autism evaluation, both of which confirmed a potential autism diagnosis. A friend with early childhood education told me to get him checked out. The speech therapist and family doctor recommended it. Why did these words finally set me over the edge? Yet for some reason, the words sank deeper. My fortitude over this possible diagnosis was like a toy boat in the bathtub slowly filling with water as my child poured more and more over it.

These words were the words that made it hit the porcelain bottom.

My child likely has autism.

My heart quickened in my chest. The woman on the other line continued to tell me about their program: *two months of intensive coaching for parents with a variety of specialists certain days of the week to help with speech, behavior, and social skills.* My breath felt shallow.

"Is this something you'd be interested in?" she asked.

I looked up. Daniel sat in the living room working on his phone while bouncing a twin on his knee. The young girl helping out that day scooted around me with the other twin beside her and my oldest bouncing behind her.

I took a deep breath. *I can't fall apart now.* I nodded my head, but she couldn't see me. "Yes... yes, I would like that."

Later that week, as I edited a story in the office, I heard Daniel's voice raise in the living room.

I didn't have to look to know what scene played in the living room. Our potentially autistic child hit his brother in the side of the head every few minutes because he had no other way of communicating. Next, I heard him shake the rabbit cage and laugh when Daniel told him to stop.

I heard the quiver in Daniel's voice. "Please, please stop!"

I closed the laptop and stepped out to the kitchen. "Alright boys," I called out. "Start cleaning up the toys." Then I reached out to Daniel.
"Can you help me?"

He walked down the hall, our oldest trailing behind. I peeked past my husband's arm and smiled at my son. "Honey, can you please go help your brothers clean? Mommy and Daddy need to talk for a moment."

He nodded and disappeared back down the hall.

A Mother Held

I turned to look up at my husband. "You want to join me while I tidy up the twins' room?"

He sighed. "I'm not feeling well."

"I know," I murmured. I straightened out the bedding, even though the twins would soon be in here wrinkling it up at nap time. I had no intention of lecturing him. I didn't have a plan at that moment because my own chest felt the pressure of grief, fear, and unknowns bombarding me as well. "What's wrong?" I already knew the answer. It's the same reason my patience had thinned, the same reason my voice raised more often. I looked him in the eye as I waited for his answer.

He ran a hand through his dark hair. "I'm just stressed."

I nodded. "What are you stressed about?" My stomach twisted. I knew why, and I didn't want to hear those words become verbalized.

He swallowed. "It's just... he's driving me insane. He won't leave his brother alone. He just keeps hitting him, and he doesn't listen to me."

"I know. It's because..." I rolled my lips. I forced myself to look him in the eyes. We had used this term together so often lately, yet now it stuck in my throat. "Autistic children have trouble communicating. He has no words, and he has no other way of communicating than hitting."

"Yeah." He gripped the foot of the bed and leaned over it. "I'm just..." His head fell. His shoulders crumpled. "I'm just so scared," he cried. "What if he never gets better? What if this is our whole life now? I love him, and I'm scared for him." He quietly wept.

My lip trembled. Tears prodded behind my own eyes. These were the words I didn't dare voice because I knew I'd be in the same position as my husband right now—doubled over, weeping uncontrollably. I took a deep breath. *I can't fall apart—not yet. He needs me.* I heard the siblings begin to squabble in the living room down the hall. *And they need me too.*

The words I had spoken to my friend a few days prior rumbled in my mind. I told her that we can't borrow trouble from tomorrow—we have no idea what it will bring. You need to look at today, at this moment, and see what God is calling you to do.

Those weren't my wise words. They were the gentle words of Jesus to the crowds of desperate people standing before him at the foot of the grassy mount when he preached, looking at the dappled flowers and well-fed birds that God provided for. *Don't worry about clothes and food, for your Heavenly Father knows you need them. Therefore, don't worry about tomorrow.*

Those words came back to me as I gazed at my hurting husband. I stepped onto the bed and took his chin in my hands, guiding his eyes back up to mine. "I know, I fear that too. But we don't know what tomorrow will bring. What we do know is that we have a beautiful, sweet, happy, loving, funny boy with us."

My husband nodded and wiped his eyes. "He's so sweet," he whispered. "I love the way he grins."

I smiled. "I do too. We only have today, what's right before us. And right now we have a son with a potential autism diagnosis who needs our help learning to communicate. He needs our patience and guidance."

His face twisted again. "I feel so bad I yelled at him," he murmured.

I squeezed his hand. "I know, I do it too. It's hard. But what we can do is show him what to do when we hurt someone."

He nodded and hugged me. "Thank you, dear. I love you. You're such a good mom and wife."

I blinked my tears away. He didn't know it at that moment, but I needed those words I had spoken too. I wasn't some strong preacher with my head held high. I struggled to believe in those promises, and I shared my anxieties about the future. The words I spoke came with trembling, with a faith that cried, "Help my unbelief." That's all I could do—preach to my own heart what I knew to be true and pray that God would carry me where my faith fell short.

    I pulled back from my husband and smiled at him. "You are too. God gave us this boy, not to watch us grapple and struggle, but because he knew we were the best parents for him. He will provide what we need to care for him; he promises."

    I whispered a prayer in my mind as the words left my mouth. *I believe; help my unbelief. Keep my eyes on today.*

    Later the following week, I put my little ones to bed. Within minutes, I heard one child cry out, and I knew why without seeing or asking. My suspected autistic child had hit his brother while he tried to sleep. This had become our new routine as of a few weeks prior.

    I plodded down the hallway, agitation roiling in my chest. I opened the door and asked the routine question to the crying child. "What happened?"

    With tears streaming down his face, he pointed at his brother. I clenched my teeth and asked, "Did you hit your brother?"

    He put his fingers in his mouth and laughed, then ran across the room.

    I gathered up the crying brother's blankets. "C'mon, let's go to Mommy and Daddy's room." I led him across the hall and tucked him into my bed. We'd put him back once everyone had fallen asleep.

    As I closed my bedroom door, the crying echoed under the closed door to the children's room. The agitation in my heart melted into a heaviness. As a frown fought against my lips, I turned inside the children's bedroom and found the son who had hit his brother curled up by the door weeping and pointing in the direction his brother had gone.

    I shook my head. "I'm sorry, you hit him. I can't let you hit him." I took his hand and led him to his bed, a deep pout drawing his bottom lip out. He curled up on his side and sniffed, pulling his stuffed bunny in closer. I knelt by the bed and put my forehead to his. "I love you. Please stop hitting your brother, then he won't have to leave." My throat hurt. I kissed his forehead. I rubbed his hair.

"Goodnight," I whispered.

He looked up and gave me a weak smile, then tucked his hand under his head to sleep.

I can't break down now. I stiffened my lip and padded down the hallway to the office. I opened the computer, where two information packets for the autism program sat minimized in the corner. I opened one up in the background and remembered the other links the administrator had provided in her email. Two online courses, and one free box of toys for autistic children to sign up for. I scrolled through phrases such as Increasing Your Child's Attention to People, Recognizing Autism in Toddlers, and What Does Unusual Behavior in Toddlers with Autism Look Like? I thought of my whimpering child. Tears pricked my eyes like needles as I began to fill out the form.

Oh God, I prayed. *I can't hold it together. I can't do this. I'm so scared.* I took a breath and leaned back in my chair. I saw my oldest running in the field with a wide grin on his face and his father chasing him with outstretched arms. I closed my eyes. Tears ran down my cheeks. *Keep my eyes on today, Jesus, one step at a time.* I prayed these words knowing that it wasn't all up to me to keep my eyes on him—the Holy Spirit would be the one to lift my gaze day after day.

19
Given to Us and For Us

These times we know much evil, little good
To steady us in faith
And comfort when our losses press
Hard on us, and we choose,
In panic or despair or both,
To keep what we will lose.
For we are fallen like the trees, our peace
Broken, and so we must
Love where we cannot trust,
Trust where we cannot know,
And must await the wayward-coming grace
That joins living and dead,
Taking us where we would not go—
Into the boundless dark.
When what was made has been unmade
The Maker comes to His work.

— Wendell Berry[25]

My two-year-old son bolts down the dock at top speed during high tide. My heart catches in my chest. Panic freezes my limbs. I envision his tiny body flying over the edge and into the dark, white-capped waves. I straighten my arm and yell at my husband: "Daniel! Get him!"

Daniel is already on his feet. He runs down the dock and grabs our son a foot from the edge. I dig my fingers into the sand

---
[25] Berry, *A Timbered Choir*, 74.

with my shoulders hunched up around my jaw as Daniel leads him back down the dock. I hear him tell our son why he can never do that again.

This isn't the first time our boy has heard this message. When we return here each day after we walk on the old train tracks, he attempts to sprint down the dock. Sometimes, he slips past us and runs down to the edge, but so far this year the water has remained low tide. And just like every other time he's listened to this lecture from Daniel or me, he walks proudly with a big smile on his face, still trying to wriggle free. He still doesn't get it, and his provisional neuro-divergence diagnosis may be a figure in that.

A thought barrels through my mind: *I'm going to lose him. I'm going to lose my adventurous child—and it will be all my fault.*

This isn't simply catastrophic thinking after a one-time event. Rather, this is the same child who sprints down the driveway regularly toward the busy road at the bottom of the hill. He still eats sand and rocks and climbs furniture to the highest shelf in the closet. If I look away from him for even a few seconds, he disappears. He'll dart into the woods without ever looking back.

All these moments rattle through my brain like a pickup truck as he toddles off the dock.

My heart plummets into my stomach like he's already dead—because, if his life relies on my abilities, he could be.

It's been another one of those days—a day where I seemingly never stopped moving, never stopped answering questions or text messages, and my feet now throbbed as a result of it. Yet as I moved towards the living room, I heard that little voice of my tuckered-out adventurous boy calling for "mum." With a tired smile, I stepped into his room, careful not to bump him into the door.

A Mother Held

"Do you need to be tucked in?" I asked.

He grinned and scampered back to his bed, pulling himself up over the edge with his belly. He rolled onto his back and beamed up at me as I brought the sheets and duvet up under his chin.

Without any prompting, he raised his arms and wrapped them around my neck. He tugged my head down between that small space between his neck and shoulder and nestled his head into mine. I remained there for a moment, then pulled away to say goodnight.

He looked up at me with that smile full of little teeth, then tugged me back in for another hug. This time, his grip didn't relax right away, but he held on tight—and I took a moment to breathe in his scent and feel my angst from the day melt away.

One morning, I peeled off my yellow, rubber gloves to wipe my forehead with the back of my hand. I had neglected cleaning the windows because of my deep-seated hatred for it and made excuse upon excuse as to why it couldn't be done this week or next. But now, with my husband preparing to replace the broken screens, I knew I had to finally scrub the mildew, dust, and questionable grime from the sills and panes while the homeschooled girl took care of the boys.

Looking for a break, I went on a scavenger hunt for my water bottle. After I retrieved it from the kitchen, I paused in the hallway to peek at the voices I heard in the twins' room. I tilted, barely able to peer between the wall and doorway to see inside the room.

The girl stood in front of one of the beds, looking at my adventurous child. He bounced on the bed and flapped his arms—the way he always did—in just a t-shirt and a diaper. She picked up his pants and held them in front of him. "C'mon, show me how you can put your pants on," she said.

A bit of shame pricked my heart. I had yet to teach him how to put his clothes on. With homeschooling my oldest, cleaning, playing, folding, and cooking, responsibilities like this often got thrown to the side. I shifted my weight, waiting for her to provide the help he would inevitably need.

My son stopped dancing and looked at the pants. She pressed them closer to his hands. "Here you go, you can do it."

He reached out and took the pants from her hand and plopped down to his bum. I leaned closer to watch. He leaned back against the headboard and stretched his skinny legs out in front of himself. He squirmed his left leg in, but the right foot got caught. He let go of the pants and yelled.

"No, it's okay! You can do it. You often get stuck here, but you always get your foot through eventually."

He looked at her in dismay then put his head back down to work. He wriggled and puffed, and his toes finally made their way through.

"Alright," she said, reaching out her hands. "Stand up!"

He carefully stood to his feet, toddling slightly. A smile pulled at my lips as he bent over and took the waist of his pants, hauling them up over his knees and diapered bottom. I pushed away from the wall and padded down the hall toward them. The young girl looked up and smiled at me. "There! Show Mommy how you can finish pulling up your pants!"

I crossed my arms with my gloves tucked inside my elbow and widened my eyes expectantly. "Yes! Show me!"

He grinned—that kind of grin that creases his whole face—and plucked at his pants until they came up nearly as high as his diaper, though the elastic waist was ruffled quite a bit. The young girl laughed. "He usually has trouble with the waist," she said, straightening it out. "There! Now you can go play!"

I watched him hop down from the bed and run out the door, the young girl not far behind. I smiled to myself as I finished scrubbing the windows.

A Mother Held

A couple of hours later, I heard her call out that it was lunchtime. Before I even made it to the kitchen, she stood at the cupboard laying slices of cheese on whole wheat bread to make grilled cheese sandwiches, chatting away with my boys about the importance of sitting with bums on chairs so they don't tumble to the floor.

Another day we sat at our beloved shore again, wading in the waves and sorting through the rocks and shells. My adventurous child grinned and clambered over the large, jagged rocks. Each time he mounted an especially large one, he stood up as tall as he could and exclaimed, "Eh up igh!" At first, I just watched him from my spot, but then he adventured much further than I would have liked.

A part of me wanted to call him back, envisioning his body crashing and getting scraped up. But another part of me that I had dimmed since childhood that love scaling rocks and imagining myself climbing a mountain like Bilbo and the dwarves, beckoned me to follow. So I did.

Him with his bare feet and me with my hot pink sneakers, we climbed over every flat and craggy rock, passing over washed-up wood and fishing gear, until we made it to the edge with the tall grass. I watched his chubby self grapple with the crumbling edge until he began to run through the sand reeds. Adrenaline and excitement coursed through me as I climbed up behind him and followed.

Our Sunday mornings are spent at church. We talk with beloved friends, hear Scripture preached, worship God by song, partake of the sacraments, and chase our adventurous child between the seats while he tries to suck the ink out of pens. We try to sandwich all three of them between my husband and me, but he still slips through our legs and under chairs beyond our reach to scribble on the hymnals or carpeted floor.

During the singing one Sunday, my adventurous child found a small pencil and an offering envelope under one of the seats. When I glanced over to make sure the pencil tip hadn't stabbed into anything like a weapon, I saw the woman next to us—who we barely knew—remove a sheet of paper from her purse and lay it down on the seat for my boy. She gently took his pencil and drew big swirling loops on the page, then handed it back to him with a smile. As he peeked up at her from the corner of his eye and gently retrieved the pencil from her hand, tears prodded the corners of my eyes.

The same day at the shoreline that my adventurous one ran down the dock with the sloshing high tide, he climbs around the large rocks to wade in at the water's edge. Daniel and I sit on the edge of the dock, guarding it from little feet trying to bolt past us. While my husband shares about his work day, I watch the little one from the corner of my eye. He's usually so balanced and loves to play on the rocks, but today the water rolls in higher than usual and his legs look wobbly. I lean ahead. "Daniel, Daniel, he's going down!"

My adventurous child falls to his knees, his face inches from the water as waves lap up. His arms buckle.

Daniel shoves off the dock and sprints through the waves, shoes and all, and grabs our son from the cold water. He wails and rubs his face with his pudgy hands, droplets of salt water dripping from his hair. I run to them and examine his face closely. His face is mostly dry, and the water in his hair splashed up from my husband's large feet pounding through the waves.

A Mother Held

I hold him close and soothe him, then tuck him in the stroller with Daniel's dry sweater while the other two boys get ready to return home too.

By the time we parade up the hill, it seems our sweet boy has recovered. He beams at our concerned faces and giggles at his brothers' antics, kicking his sopping feet in excitement. As we walk up the driveway, scenes of all the people who look out for my adventurous child replay through my mind: His older brother lifting him to the trampoline, the young girl making his lunch, his grandmother distracting him from a head-banging tantrum on her kitchen floor, his twin bringing him a toy and hugging him after he stubbed his toe, and Grandpère giving him a ride in his front-end loader around the sawmill.

These mundane moments fill our ordinary months, but I saw something different than I'd noticed before. The many hands and feet that care for my adventurous child and the many hearts that tenderly adore him. This is my adventurous child, given not just to me—not just for me to hike up my sleeves, grit my teeth, and raise all on my own—but to *us*. To my husband, to his siblings, to his grandparents, to the church, and to our friends. This is what it takes to raise a child: Numerous hands held together like a net or threaded basket, lifting him toward what is good, true, and beautiful.

But even more, I'm realizing that this child isn't just given *to* us but *for* us. He's not just teaching me my need for others, but opening my eyes to the world I often pass by. When my eyes are glued to a screen to answer messages or refresh an app, when I assume I'm too busy to slow down for a hug, he reminds me otherwise. He bends low to the ground and cries out, "Aaannnt!" He won't relent until I put away my device and kneel with him to watch the little black critter drag a crumb of food across the pavement and over blades of grass back to his hole. He notices every single insect that crosses his path and makes a point of declaring it to anyone who will listen.

The reason why my adventurous child runs isn't to disobey or to drive me bananas, but because he's so incredibly curious about this world around him and wants to discover it for himself—not through a screen. His lack of awareness makes that dangerous for him at times, but I believe God gave me this child because of all the times I've prayed, "Teach me to slow down and see your glory all around me." That's what my adventurous child is doing each time he runs to the forest and I follow him or whenever he runs to waves and tilts down to examine the way the rocks look under them. He's not another struggle to my day, but a chance to find God at the level of a child filled with wonder.

A few days later, I stand in the garage entryway. The kiddos bring their bikes and buckets to the garage door, tossing them in on the cement floor. As the last toy gets shuffled inside, I click the button to bring the door down. The kids are close, but I don't worry—it has a sensor that causes it to stop and return to the top whenever someone crosses underneath while it's moving down. It's more of a nuisance.

As the door comes down, I notice my adventurous child laughing and running for the threshold. I groan inside, wondering how long this will take. I call for him to stop, but he doesn't. As I hear his twin brother cry out, I look at where they stand. As my son runs to go under the door, his twin brother wraps his arms around his adventurous sibling and pulls him backwards. My boy hits, squirms, and yells in frustration, but his twin sibling continues shrieking and pulling him back to where he believes he'll be safer.

A Mother Held

As for me—I'm too emotional to know how to react; I simply smile. One thing I do know: This boy was given *to* all of us and given *for* each of us.

20

A Life Lived Out of Doors— Despite the Dangers

> *One other thing [a mother] will do, but very rarely, and with tender filial reverence ... she will point to some lovely flower or gracious tree, not only as a beautiful work, but a beautiful thought of God, in which we may believe He finds continual pleasure, and which He is pleased to see his human child rejoice in. Such a seed of sympathy with the Divine thought sown in the heart of the child is worth many of the sermons the man may listen to hereafter, much of the 'divinity' he may read.*
>
> — Charlotte Mason, *Home Education*[26]

The sun flickered through the moving curtain as I pressed up from the bed to the sound of soft giggles.

I ran a hand through my short hair with a sleepy smile and padded across the hall to the room where two of my children sleep. As I creaked the door open, they both popped their heads up from behind the unmade bed and beamed at me.

"Who wants to cuddle?" I whispered.

---

[26] Charlotte Mason, *Home Education*, 5th ed., vol. 1 (Living Book Press, 2017), 79–80.

A Mother Held

They both scrambled on top of the wrinkled sheets and crawled over to the bed closest to me. As I lay on my side, one child curved his back into my belly and nestled his head under my chin. The other stood in front of us from the floor, his big grin stretching and creasing his face.

"How are you this morning?" I asked, holding his hand.

As he giggled bashfully and shook his head, a dark dot in the crest of his ear caught my eye. I held his arm a bit more firmly and tugged his body closer to me. I propped myself up on my elbow and gently pulled his ear closer to my face. A moose tick had latched itself to the inside of his earlobe. I cringed as I ripped it from his skin. The snuggles were forced to end abruptly as I took the nasty critter to the bathroom to be flushed.

Watching it spiral down the porcelain bowl, the thought flickered through me that we could simply remain inside rather than go outdoors. Ticks pass diseases, dangerous diseases. Was it worth the risk? Checking each night didn't seem to matter, because I somehow always missed one and found it hours later already attached. I couldn't protect my three children from contracting Lyme disease.

I shook my head as if the thought could fall out. Unreasonable, I knew it. But could I prevent it in other ways? Force them to wear long sleeves all summer long with pants tucked into socks? Keep them out of the woods and tall grass at all costs?

A summer prior I almost swore off outdoor play. With an adventurous child who loved to shove rocks and handfuls of sand in his mouth, images of him choking and me struggling to clear his airway in time filled my head. I would lose him, one of the beloved sons I received after two miscarriages.

He still put rocks in his mouth, and now the ticks were worse than they ever had been. My arms aren't long enough, my eyes not quick enough, my ears not vigilant enough to catch it all. I can't save him—I'm too limited. Is it worth it?

Of course, little boys who love the outdoors won't be convinced of rules like these, and I knew it was unreasonable of me to ask. Later that day, we played outside in the sun, laying in the tall weeds my husband had yet to weed-whack around the slide and swings. I knew a pre-nap tick-check was on the schedule after lunch.

When I called them to the steps, the three boys ran like little chicks through the porch and flapped into their seats at the table, the twins needing a bit of help climbing into their booster seats. As I snapped up their buckles and slid their trays into place, I smiled at their grimy, blackened feet. I could see each swirl in their heels, like lines on a map, from the dirt embedded in their soft skin. Their toenails finished with a ragged black line at the tip where dirt collected underneath.

I recognized this all too well. I knew another child whose heels appeared dipped in charcoal every summer.

"Your sheets are full of dirt!" my mother said, pulling the new fitted sheet down on the mattress. "How do they get so muddy? Are you wearing shoes out there?"

I told her yes and showed her my flip-flops, with the indented and browned heel for proof. She shook her head and laughed. "You need to wash your feet each night before getting into bed from now on."

Being the obedient child that I was, each night I shimmied up the pine cabinet that held the sink. I sat cross-legged on the wooden counter and turned the tap on both cold and hot, my hand waiting beneath the flow until it reached the right temperature. Then I grabbed a face cloth from the basket behind me, rubbed the bar of soap over it, and stuck my feet in the white sink.

Swirls of gritty dirt whirled around the porcelain, sometimes splashing up to the mirror-like faucet.

A Mother Held

I scrubbed my feet until they appeared peachy again—though there always seemed to remain a sliver of a fragment of dirt in the swirls of my heels.

My mom believed in the power and importance of nature, and she sent me out there any time I could. When I was younger, she built snowmen and castles in the snow with me or brought me with her to arrange flower beds. We spent many evenings in the horse barn, saddling up and riding through the paths in the woods. As I got older, she let me play further from the house and explore the ponds and forest close to our house, including a white bridge for me to cross over the stream that tumbled into a waterfall.

She didn't like the blackened sheets, but she knew what was most important—a life spent outdoors, even when bits of hay and slime from the pond accompanied it. She knew it mattered, not just so that her daughter could distinguish between a frog and a toad, but for something more important: for a life well-lived and flourishing, like those tall trees I climbed in our front yard.

This year I read *Home Education* by Charlotte Mason in preparation for homeschooling. I expected it to be a drawn-out, slavish work of necessity; though passionate about homeschooling, the thought of actually following through overwhelmed me. I also figured someone who wrote six volumes at the turn of the twentieth century couldn't have written very compelling words. Yet it turned out to awaken a passion for the wonders of motherhood in me.

In this volume, Mason dedicated an entire chapter to the importance of a life lived out of doors. She wrote, "Let them once get in touch with Nature, and a habit is formed which will be a source of delight through life. We were all meant to be naturalists, each in his degree, and it is inexcusable to live in a world so full of the marvels of plant and animal life and to care for none of these things."[27] Mason considered it a pitiable idea that a child may go his entire life and not be able to recognize a bumblebee.

In practice, I learned first from my mother the need for a life of grass between our toes, dirt smudged on our faces, and tree bark glued to our hands. Rather than making trips to the zoo, my mother caught me by the shoulders and pointed out the window whenever an otter, beaver, porcupine, or squirrel toddled through our property. She taught me not only how to catch frogs and snakes but how to respect them too.

I walked with my oldest son one day along the forest edge of our yard, and I asked him questions about what we saw. *What do these pine needles feel like? What color are these flowers?* and so on. As we passed by a group of mushrooms, I asked him if he thought maybe grasshoppers used them as beds.

As the words left my mouth, a memory came rushing in like a wind at my back—of my younger self, maybe five or older, walking with my grandmother through the forest. We passed by a stump with chips of a pine cone on top, and she slowed me down in front of it and pointed at it with her frail hand. "You see that there, Lara?" she asked. "That's where some squirrels had a good meal together."

With that memory, another one pooled into my mind: My mother walking me through the forest paths in autumn, where our horse trails were completely covered in gold and orange. We had a bag to collect leaves to press in the big books at home—the same books where we had pressed tiny violets from the previous summer. She taught me to notice the beauty around me.

---

[27] Charlotte Mason, *Home Education*, 61.

A Mother Held

She never read or wrote poetry, but she taught me to see the poetry of nature as she dug her hands into the earth to array flowers in just the right way.

All these years later, Charlotte Mason taught me the philosophy behind what had been ingrained into my nature all those years ago. As anxiety crept into my heart about all the dangers that lurked outside, their lessons came together in my mind to remind me of the greater work that comes from a life lived out of doors. Mason, however, added another layer my mother had yet to see: that nature forms greater adoration, faith, and righteous fear in the human heart that restlessly longs for its Creator. And I believe God used the faithfulness of my mother to build that faith in me for my own life.

21
On Growing Old, Being Loved, and Becoming Real

> And you as well must die, beloved dust,
> And all your beauty stand you in no stead;
> This flawless, vital hand, this perfect head,
> This body of flame and steel, before the gust
> Of Death, or under his autumnal frost,
> Shall be as any leaf, be no less dead
> Than the first leaf that fell,—this wonder fled.
>
> — Edna St. Vincent Millay, And You As Well Must Die, Beloved Dust

There was a time in my life when I ate a cinnamon roll coated in icing daily and had ice cream for "breakfast dessert." I wasn't too concerned about healthy eating or what sugar did to my body. But in seventh grade, my unhealthy habits began to catch up to me. Rather than being a slim pole bean as I always was, I started gaining weight. I didn't think much of the weight until a friend brought it up at a sleepover. As she eyed my silhouette in the doorway, she said, "Lara, you're starting to get a belly."

She probably didn't mean anything by it, but after that day I became obsessed with looking at my stomach in the mirror. *Is it bigger? Is it any smaller?* I tried exercising in the evenings, but it never seemed to make a difference. Eventually, I gave up and started wearing loose clothing that kept my belly covered.

A Mother Held

In eleventh grade, I changed my habits. I started eating "clean" (no processed foods or sugar) and exercised daily for an hour. One day when I lifted my shirt to look at my stomach, I found it flat. No longer slightly bulged or rounded, but flat, with some muscle beginning to show.

After struggling with feeling "fat" throughout most of high school, you would think this would have come as a relief to me. It didn't. Instead, it led to further anxiety. *What if I lose this?* I restricted my diet further and exercised more as a guardrail to help when I accidentally messed up my limited diet. If I ever had an unhealthy meal or ate a treat as small as a cookie, I either lay in bed fending off panic attacks or dripping in sweat from an intense cardio workout.

When I looked at the other girls in my class with their flowing, styled hair, smooth skin, brand-name clothes (that I often couldn't afford), and fashion-model-worthy makeup routines (that my skin couldn't tolerate), I saw my flat stomach as the only attractive aspect of myself. When the boys laughed at the girl who made the floor shake when she walked across the classroom, and I saw the girls who didn't have the same body shape as everyone else sitting alone in the cafeteria, I knew that if I ever stood a chance at maintaining friendships and romantic relationships, I had to do everything I could to keep my stomach flat.

In 2016, I married my high school sweetheart at the summer camp we both worked for. I believed I had overcome the hardest passage of all; I kept my weight down to secure a husband. But the obsessive beast didn't go away, and that young girl at the altar had no idea what age and motherhood would do to her body.

"I think I need to invest in some wrinkle cream," I said to Daniel as I stared in the bathroom mirror one night.

He laughed. "Why do you need wrinkle cream?"

"To prevent wrinkles," I replied tersely. Doesn't he know how this works? I patted my hair. "I think I need to start dyeing my hair too. The grays are becoming more and more unruly."

He smiled and kissed my forehead. "I believe you're beautiful just the way you are."

I groaned and rolled my eyes. Of course, he'd say that. That's what he vowed to do at the altar.

I smiled warily. "You know you did this to me, right? I didn't have gray hair until I married you and we had kids."

We laughed because it's been a running joke since I found my first gray hair a few weeks after our wedding. But deep down, there was a part of me that bitterly believed it to be true.

My body, though still young, is already full of signs of aging. Wrinkles and gray hair. Joints that creak and groan. Skin that dries out the moment the weather changes. Each day, it seems like I'm finding another part of my body that resembles my mother. I remember looking at her hands with their protruding veins as a child and asking in wonder, "Will mine do that?!" I can already see it happening. She complained of her arms randomly going to sleep; now mine do that while I work out or when I'm trying to fall asleep.

Childbearing also took its toll on my body. My lower back easily becomes sore after carrying my firstborn and twin boys in my womb. My stomach looks like a parched lake with its stretch marks and will likely never be completely flat like it was in college. I have a scar where my twins were surgically removed from me when my body was unable to push them out. I wear my knees out bending down and driving cars on the floor.

We often joke and poke fun at our families to blame them for our messy homes and decrepit bodies, and deep down perhaps we truly do blame them to some extent. If it weren't for being married to a sinner (and me being a sinner as well) and birthing multiple children, maybe I wouldn't look so haggardly. I look at the younger girls around me and go home to pinch the loose skin above my waistband. I examine the random hairs that grow on my chin and the ever-flourishing crop of gray hair taking over my head.

A Mother Held

It's not just my physical body either; as I said before, marriage and motherhood caused sins I didn't know resided in my heart to bob up to the surface. I didn't realize how angry or selfish I could be until I had four other people asking things of me. Perhaps you see this in yourself too. In the solitude of your mind, you catch yourself wondering how much your family has worn your mind and body sooner than you anticipated. "This flawless, vital hand, this perfect head, / This body of flame and steel," as Edna St. Vincent Millay describes it, is suddenly not so resilient after all.

Yet one day as I read *The Velveteen Rabbit* to my oldest on the couch—and my legs were inevitably going to sleep from my son sitting on my lap—I couldn't help but wonder: What if we flipped the narrative?

In *The Velveteen Rabbit* by Margery Williams Bianco, the stuffed rabbit asked the large toy pony (referred to as the Skin Horse) about being real. The rabbit desperately wanted to be real, but it seemed to him that being real meant having wind-up keys and gears. But the skin horse had a different reply.

> "What is Real?" asked the Rabbit one day, when they were lying side by side near the nursery fender, before Nana came to tidy the room. "Does it mean having things that buzz inside you and a stick-out handle?"
>
> "Real isn't how you are made," said the Skin Horse. "It's a thing that happens to you. When a child loves you for a long, long time, not just to play with, but really loves you, then you become Real."
>
> "Does it hurt?" asked the Rabbit.
>
> "Sometimes," said the Skin Horse, for he was always truthful. "When you are Real you don't mind being hurt."
>
> "Does it happen all at once, like being wound up," he asked, "or bit by bit?"
>
> "It doesn't happen all at once," said the Skin Horse. "You become. It takes a long time. That's why it doesn't happen often to people who break easily, or have sharp edges, or who have to be carefully kept. Generally, by the time you are Real, most of your hair has been loved off, and your eyes drop out and you get loose in the joints and very shabby. But these things don't matter at all, because once you are Real you can't be ugly, except to people who don't understand."

I looked down at my stomach, feeling the folds of skin hanging over my waistband that years ago weren't there. Reading this children's story, I can't help but wonder, *What if these stretch marks, incision lines, creaking knees, and graying hair are all signs and reminders of being loved and loving those dearest to me? What if what the world tells me is ugliness and unbecoming is what makes me beautiful to those who matter most? What if the drawing of all these sins to the surface is God reshaping me into the likeness of Christ?*

I'm beginning to believe that what my children will carry with them, and my husband will remember of me won't be how pristine I kept my appearance but the time we spent together playing, laughing, running, and tumbling. They will remember the games of tickle-chase, racing cars down the tracks, and reading books that are so beloved that their binding is wearing off too. I hope when they look back at my failures, they can see a mom receiving the carving knife of God in repentance and sanctification.

But what happens when all that wear and tear on our bodies isn't appreciated? When we wipe sweat from our brows after scrubbing floors only to have a child run with mucky boots down that same hallway, or when we cook a complicated meal and only hear complaints, or when all those hours we spent building block towers are utterly forgotten?

In *The Velveteen Rabbit*, the little boy who loves the rabbit gets scarlet fever. Though he recovers, the doctor orders that all the bedclothes be burned to get rid of the germs—and this includes the stuffed rabbit. He's tossed in a bag in the garden to be burned the next day. He weeps and wonders what was the point of all the pain and loss of his beauty if it all amounted to him being thrown away. Yet as his tears dampen the soil, a flower blooms and a fairy steps from it. She says she has heard the cry of the Velveteen Rabbit and she will make him into a real rabbit. The rabbit is confused because he believed he was already real, but the fairy says she will make him real to everyone.

A Mother Held

The journey that the Velveteen Rabbit embarks on reflects the Christian life; we become "real" when we first believe in Jesus, and through much wear and tear God sanctifies us to become more like Jesus until the day he draws us into his kingdom where we are made completely new and freed from the flesh—then we are made fully real. We were created for a perfect, sinless relationship with God, but sin has marred that. God makes us more and more real each day as he sanctifies us. I love what Vigen Guroian writes reflecting on this treasured story:

> The Skin Horse achieves the first stage of being real, but for all his wisdom, he cannot imagine the next stage that would make him real "forever and ever." The Velveteen Rabbit, however, is set on a path to this second kind of realness. This is by no merit of his own but rather through his intense desire to be a real rabbit, and by a Greater Love that cares for the toys in the nursery too much to allow them to be just thrown away after they are "used up."[28]

Isn't this how sanctification works? God draws out our pilgrimages toward truth, beauty, and goodness through many moments, years of living in fellowship, and times beholding his grace. We pass through fire and endure the battering of many waves on this earth until we are brought into the new heavens and earth so that when we come out on the other side, we look most beautiful to the only One who can see that inner beauty fully.

We can't force our growth through our own methods of discipline. Those who try to make themselves beautiful and holy by their own works have "lost connection with the head, from whom the whole body, supported and held together by its ligaments and sinews, grows as God causes it to grow," Paul wrote. "Such regulations indeed have an appearance of wisdom, with their self-imposed worship, their false humility and their harsh treatment of the body, but they lack any value in restraining sensual indulgence" (Col. 2:19, 23 ESV).

---

[28] Guroian, *Tending the Heart of Virtue*, 66.

Let's continue to pour ourselves out for our families from the same sacrificial love Christ showed us, who never allows his beloved ones to be forgotten or lost, even if it means we grow less and less beautiful in the world's eyes. As we do, we can trust that even if our dearest loved ones never remember or appreciate all those acts of kindness and sacrifice God is still at work through them to make us more like Christ—to make us more real—until the day he brings us home. May we each strive for the beauty of wisdom and years well spent loving those entrusted to us, not what the world demands of us.

One day, we must die, my fellow beloved dust, as Millay describes us. Though "all [our] beauty stand [us] in no stead" and "It mattering not how beautiful [we] were," Christ will bring us into a better Eden and redeem our broken selves for eternal life, which he spent an entire lifetime carving more and more into his likeness.

Epilogue: I Look Toward

Twilight and evening bell,
And after that the dark!
And may there be no sadness of farewell,
When I embark;
For tho' from out our bourne of Time and Place
The flood may bear me far,
I hope to see my Pilot face to face
When I have crost the bar.

— *Alfred, Lord Tennyson, Crossing the Bar*

I call my husband to the bedroom to go over the upcoming week's schedule. As he comes down the hall, I let myself fall backwards dramatically into the pile of clean but still unfolded sheets piled on the bed. He laughs and I let out a huff of air.

"It's another one of those weeks," I say. I hold my phone above my head and scroll through the calendar app. "Tuesday you have an appointment at the hospital with the dietician. Wednesday we have a home visit with Early Childhood Developmental Intervention. Thursday I have therapy in the morning and speech therapy for the twins in the afternoon."

He nods. "Okay, so Monday is—"

I shake my head. "No, Monday is a holiday."

"I thought Monday we started that autism program?"

"No," I reply with an amused smile. "That's next Monday."

"Every Monday?"

I nod and look toward him. "For July. Then it changes to every Wednesday through to November."

We both exchange an exhausted glance. We're grateful, but we're tired.

At 9 p.m., I walk bleary-eyed to the kitchen, covering my mouth as I yawn. My head aches from another day of breaking up fights between siblings and repeatedly tucking in little ones. Daniel opens the cupboard and reaches to the top shelf, taking out a plastic bin full of medications. As he sets it down, he reaches up again and brings down three more bottles for me.

I yawn and push two of the bottles aside. "Not these two. I take the pink ones in the morning, and I don't take the ones in the green bottle anymore."

"Oh yeah, I forgot," he replies. He picks them up in his hand and puts them back, shoving aside old medication bottles from pills we no longer took because they gave us odd side effects like diarrhea or shakiness. "Why not the green bottle anymore?"

I shrug. "They give me vivid nightmares. It's a rare side effect; the pharmacist didn't even know about it until she looked it up."

"Strange."

We down our pills to quiet our mental illnesses, brush our teeth, and crawl under the sheets together. I prop three pillows up behind me to wait for the pills to settle in my stomach to prevent acid reflux when I lay down. I slide my book out from the nightstand and click my lamp on next to me as I look toward the novel where I hope to find a bit of eternity.

A Mother Held

A few days later, we pull into the pharmacy parking lot. As the van parks, my muddy children reach out for my seat on the passenger side. "Can I come with you?!" my five-year-old calls out from the back.

I laugh and shake my head. "You're soaking wet from playing in the puddles! Mommy will just be quick."

I walk in through the glass doors and make my way to the back where the pharmacists shuffle behind their glassed-in counter, organized medication cabinets, and answer phone calls. I hear the usual mixture of French and English, which I always enjoy translating in my head (just to prove to myself I didn't forget my days of French immersion in high school).

The pharmacist's assistant sees my head and smiles. "For twin #1?" she asks. They know us here—and not just because it's a small town.

"Yup," I reply. I pass over my cards and she rings it through. I sigh in relief as yet another unexpected medical bill somehow goes through without making our debit card scream, "REJECTED!" It had times before in grocery lines at the checkout while the cashier looked perturbed. It doesn't help we had just spent over one hundred dollars the previous month on an Epipen for another child. I thank God for what he provides today.

"Alright, the pharmacist will need to speak with you," she says. "Just pop over to that next window." She didn't need to tell me; I knew the drill.

The pharmacist soon appears in front of me, holding the brown bag containing our prescription. "Twin #1 still struggling with that cough?"

I nod. "Yeah, he's coughing every night and his breath sounds rattly."

She nods as well. "We're suspecting asthma?"

"Yes, that's what the doctor thinks."

"Gotcha. Alright, well this puffer will work with the one you already have. Give this new one first so it will open up the lungs, then a minute later give the other one. You'll do this twice a day. This new one can be used as needed, just within the hours written here."

I look toward her. "Perfect. Thanks so much."

She smiles and slides the bag over to me. I gather it up and plod down to the front of the store again and out to the parking lot.

At home, I plan the logistics out in my head as I smooth peanut butter over slices of seedy bread. *After breakfast, I'll wash up Twin #1 and give him his puffer. To make sure I leave enough time, I'll wash up Twin #2 and their older brother. Then I'll go back to Twin #1 and give him the second puffer. I'll do the same at bedtime after snack.* As I handed out the lunches and looked toward each child, I made a mental note to update all the other medical professionals about his new puffer.

My mind aches at the thought of it. Another bill, another duty to remember, another issue to watch out for. For a moment, part of me feels like I'm about to crumble. Then I feel the gnawing in my stomach and remember I need to eat too. I look toward the cupboard to find my own lunch.

Later that week, I retreat to the basement, saying I need to do laundry, but, as it often is, I need to do more than dump clothes into the washing machine. I take my phone from the back pocket of my jeans and place the hamper of dirty towels on the cement floor. My fingers know the exact place the app sat, nestled into a folder on the second screen. I tap Voxer and open the chat with two writing friends who years ago had become much more than just professional acquaintances.

I never know how to start when asking for prayer, and sometimes I don't even know what I'm really asking for. I awkwardly start with, "Good morning!" and hope they are both doing well, then I proceed to word-vomit our entire journey with receiving an autism assessment for one of my boys: The hour-long calls with hundreds of assessment questions, connecting with various professionals that could assist with home visits and problem-solving, speech development and occupational therapy. All the while, little yet enormous-sounding feet pound on the ceiling above me with shrieks of excitement.

I exclaim my gratitude for all these resources available to us as I pace the floor, but my throat threatens to close off as I express my overwhelm and fears. Every "what if" that enters my mind, every symptom and sign that causes me to pause and question, and each conversation that makes me feel like crying tears of both joy and grief.

I take a breath and look toward the screen. "Anyway, all that to say, just please pray for us that we wouldn't feel so overwhelmed and for a clear mind as we go through all of this." I click the send button and close my phone. Finally, I look toward the washer to do the laundry, knowing the soothing feeling that will come as I fold tiny pants and hang button-up shirts later today.

I flip the Bible open with the ribbon bookmark to our place in Genesis. I glance over the section, Genesis 5:1–32, debating if I should skip it for this morning's devotional time with the kids. I take a breath and decide to plow forward.

"Adam was 130 years old when he fathered a son in his likeness, according to his image, and named him Seth," I begin. "Adam lived 800 years after he fathered Seth, and he fathered other sons and daughters. So Adam's life lasted 930 years—" I pause and look up at my five-year-old. "—then he died."

My oldest simply watches me with an ordinary stare as he shovels Rice Crispies in his mouth.

I continue. "Seth was 105 years old when he fathered Enosh. Seth lived 807 years after he fathered Enosh, and he fathered other sons and daughters. So Seth's life lasted 912 years—" I stop again and look up. "—then he died."

The same stare. The same unbothered complexion.

I continue on through the whole list. *He lived this many years... and then he died... he lived this many years... and then he died... and then he died... and then he died.* All except one, who was taken up to Heaven, and then he was no more.

As I finish the section, I gently shut the Bible and look up at my three boys. "Did you notice anything repeated in this section today?" I ask all of them, but I knew only my five-year-old stood a chance at answering.

He shrugs his shoulders. "I don't know."

I place my hands over the cloth-covered Bible. "Everyone had babies, lived their lives, and then they died. We all die one day; we do not live forever."

I look toward the medicine cabinet. "But if we trust in Jesus that he saved us from our sins, we will be raised again to eternal life with God."

He finishes the last bite of his cereal, a bit of milk dripping from his chin. "Can I go play now?"

I grin and look toward my Bible. "Yes, just let me pray."

Daniel rubs his face with the heels of his hands and then flops down on the bed beside me. His top arm wheels around my waist and lower back as he pulls me in tighter. The afternoon sunlight glitters a bit of gold in his brown hair. "How about we just take a nap right here?"

A Mother Held

  I smile and kiss his lips, his scratchy beard tickling my nose as I blink my burning eyes. "I'd like that."

  I rest my head against his shoulder, and in no time one of our three children trips into the room laughing and quickly scrambles onto the bed where he worms his way between us. I tuck his flaxen hair under my chin and hug him close. I close my eyes and look toward eternity.

Acknowledgements

Make a place to sit down.
Sit down. Be quiet.
You must depend upon
affection, reading, knowledge,
skill—more of each
than you have—inspiration,
work, growing older, patience,
for patience joins time
to eternity. Any readers
who like your poems,
doubt their judgment.

— Wendell Berry, How to be a Poet[29]

Y ou might notice I began this final part with the same poem I began the book with. Whereas in the beginning I sought to focus on how good writing grows out of a life lived locally with community, I want to point out here how good writing relies on depending "upon affection, reading, knowledge, skill—more of each than you have." I know this to be true, which is why this collection of essays is far from a solitary endeavor. It required the love, care, and tending to of many friends and family.

---

[29] Berry, "How to be a Poet."

A Mother Held

  To my husband, Daniel: What words are there to exclaim my love and gratitude to you? Like everyone else, you gave of yourself, your time, and our own money to make this book happen. You stand in every story, whether in the background or forefront, reflecting the love of Christ to me every step of the way. Thank you.

  To my three boys: I often think of myself as your teacher and guide, which is true, but I forget that God uses each of you to teach me truths about him, this world, and what it means to have child-like faith.

  To my mother: You heard about my dreams of writing a book at such a young age. In fact, when my second-grade teacher noticed how much I struggled with writing a story, you're the one who spent hours upon hours reading terrible stories and providing the critique and advice I needed. You're one of the people who toiled to cultivate an imagination in me. You sought to tend to this dream of mine in whatever way you could. You loved me and raised me to see the beauty, truth, and goodness all around me. I can never repay you, but I hope I can pass all this along to my own children as you did for me. Thank you.

  To my in-laws, Lisa and Armand: You never hesitated to support my work as a writer. You never critiqued me or wondered if I should get a "real job." Instead, you asked questions, sought to understand my work, and asked how you could show your support, whether by watching my children or giving financially. But even more, God used you to draw light into the shadowlands I often walked through with my anxiety and depression. Thank you for never giving up on me.

  To Carrie and Laura: Though you are my sisters-in-law, I will always consider you both to be the sisters I always longed for growing up. You likewise have mentored me, not just through words, but also by watching you live for your Savior and serve your families like him. I am so grateful that I get to call both of you not only earthly sisters, but sisters in Christ.

You both regularly checked in on me through my darkest moments as a mother, and you never ceased to forget about me or pray for me. Thank you.

To my church family: Your immediate love for us when we first started attending your church still amazes me. You are the hands and feet of Christ to not only me, but my husband and children too. I am constantly learning from each of you how to be hospitable and live as the body of Christ.

To Michelle and Megan, my two local best friends: Our chats about theology, our shared weirdness, and the hundreds of hours of counsel you have provided to me about motherhood have formed me unlike any book or podcast. I wouldn't be the woman I am today without your friendship.

To Samantha Cabrera: I'm still so stunned that you not only offered for me to be a part of your work at *Calla Press*, but also offered to publish this very collection of essays. You have made my first book publishing experience one of simply joy. You provided such wise counsel and guidance throughout this project, and I'm indebted to you for all the work you've put into this dream of mine. Thank you.

To Brianna Lambert and Brittany Allen: There are no words to thank you for all the hours you poured into this manuscript for me. You two of my closest friends; while our friendship began as one focused on writing, it quickly developed into something far deeper than that. You are the ones who lived through many of the sorrows and joys I recorded in this book and you helped me to edit them not only from a writing perspective but from a heart perspective. Thank you.

To Benjamin Vrbicek, Maggie Combs, and Callie Feyen: You are the editors who have believed in my work as a writer and have developed me in the craft over the years we've worked together. You push me to grow with honest yet kind criticism, thought-provoking prompts, and the warmest encouragement. You haven't let me remain

A Mother Held

the same as a writer, but have changed me again and again. I long to write with the same beauty, wisdom, and goodness each of you do. Thank you.

To my Savior, Redeemer, Father, Lord, and Refuge: The Son who saves me, the Father who sovereignly orchestrates, and the Spirit who counsels me: You are the foundation of this book, the reason for any light or hope within it. Without you, this would be a story of only brokenness and grief. All glory goes to you, for you are the true Author who wrote it all in your books from eternity past.

About the Author

Lara d'Entremont is first a wife to Daniel and a mom to three little wildlings. While the wildlings snore, she designs websites and edits for a variety of writers, but her first love is writing—whether it be personal essays, creative nonfiction, or fantasy novels.

She desires to weave the stories between faith and fiction, theology and praxis, for women who feel as if these two pieces of them are always at odds.

Lara is an editor for *Calla Press*, a staff writer for *Gospel-Centered Discipleship*, and a regular contributor to *Well-Watered Women*. Her writing can be found in *Christianity Today*, *Mere Orthodoxy*, *Modern Reformation*, *Common Good Magazine*, *Risen Motherhood*, *The Rabbit Room*, and many others. You are welcome to visit her online home at https://laradentremont.com/.